Folgore da San Gimignano and his Followers: The Complete Poems

Medieval and Renaissance
Texts and Studies

Volume 541

Folgore da San Gimignano and his Followers: The Complete Poems

Translated by

Fabian Alfie

Arizona Center for Medieval & Renaissance Studies

Tempe, Arizona

2019

Arizona Center
for Medieval &
Renaissance Studies

Published by ACMRS (Arizona Center for Medieval and Renaissance Studies)
Tempe, Arizona

∞
This book is made to last. It is set in Adobe Caslon Pro,
smyth-sewn and printed on acid-free paper to library specifications.
Printed in the United States of America

Table of Contents

Introduction: Folgore da San Gimignano and His Followers, Cenne da la Chitarra and Pietro dei Faitinelli

When modern-day readers think of the Middle Ages, they often call to mind stylized images of feudal life: lords and ladies in sumptuous castles, hunts with fierce hounds, feasts around roaring fires, knights jousting, trumpeters and troubadours, courtly attitudes, and courteous behaviors. The poetry of Folgore da San Gimignano (ca. 1265–75/ca. 1332) portrays such an idealized view. He composed three *corone* (singular, *corona*)—extended poems that employ sonnets as stanzas—that depict the days of the week, the months of the year, and an allegorical sequence about the vesting of a young knight. In his *corona* of the months, he casts a group of real-life individuals in fictitious courtly settings, and he describes them passing the time together in fine clothes, enjoying the pleasures of nobility, and falling in love. His *corona* of the days of the week is very similar to that of the months. Yet modern-day readers will also be familiar with a view of the Middle Ages diametrically opposed to Folgore's, one that emphasizes the poverty, filth, and stench of the times. The Aretine poet, Cenne da la Chitarra (d. ca. 1334), painted the negative portrait of the times by parodying Folgore's *corona* of the months of the year. Throughout his sonnet cycle, Cenne replaces Folgore's pleasurable activities with annoying ones; he describes the cold and mud of winter, and the members of his imaginary court lack money and wear threadbare attire. It has been said that Folgore's lyrics constitute the fourteenth-century "dream" of the medieval nobility, while Cenne's response comprises the "reality" of everyday life.[1] The poetry of both writers, however, is not as simple as it may first appear. A third poet, Pietro dei Faitinelli (ca. 1285–1290/1349) takes inspiration from Folgore's political writings, underscoring Folgore's engagement with the society of his age. Each in their own way, the three poets write incisive commentaries on contemporary life.

---

[1] Mario Marti, "Il 'sogno' di Folgore e la 'realtà' di Cenne," in *Cultura e stile nei poeti giocosi del tempo di Dante* (Pisa: Nistri-Lischi, 1953): 131–52.

Most of what is known about Folgore's biography comes from the registers of the commune of San Gimignano. In a document dated 25 January 1295, his name appears as part of a group of soldiers who accompanied Count Orsello to the Papal court; since he was already engaged in military service, the poet must have been born between 1265 and 1275.[2] In 1305, the city of San Gimignano reimbursed Folgore of the twenty-four *soldi* he spent travelling to and from the warfront at Pistoia. Twice during the following year, in July and again in August, San Gimignano paid him for several days of military service.[3] The registers from later decades add the title *dominus* ("sir" or "lord"), which suggests that Folgore had risen in rank to knighthood. Nicolino Applauso has recently discovered three other documents of Folgore's life. On 24 May 1308, Folgore acted as a messenger who brought news about the war between San Gimignano and Volterra, and two others, dated 1312, mention his military assistance to Florence during Henry VII's siege.[4] These newly discovered documents demonstrate him to be engaged in the military struggles between San Gimignano and other communes. In an archival document of the year 1332, Sir Folgore's children are enumerated as his heirs, implying that the poet had already died. The last historical reference to Folgore is found in an archive of 1367, as the children of his son Stefano sought to receive their inheritance ("heredi Stefani quondam domini Iacobi vocati Folgori de S. Gem."). The latter document reveals that the poet's official name was Iacobo but that he was commonly known by his nickname Folgore ("splendor").

Throughout his poetic corpus Folgore evokes the mores of an earlier age. By the start of the fourteenth century, the social, economic, and political societies of the Italian communes had long ceased following a courtly, feudal organization. The city-states of Italy were prospering, fueled by manufacturing, commerce, and international shipping.[5] The mercantile enterprises of the cities required capitalization, so vast amounts of wealth were exchanged through the lending of money. The economic boom brought social changes and inspired internal migration, as noble families moved to the cities, bringing with them funding-streams of rents from their territories; they then lent at interest, thus supporting new enterprises in an ever-growing economic cycle.[6] Non-noble merchants also attained high levels of prosperity and, hence, acquired the influence and prestige equaling or surpassing that of the aristocracy of earlier centuries. Indeed, it is

[2] Giovanni Caravaggi, *Folgore da S. Gimignano* (Milano: Ceschina, 1960): 38–39.

[3] The documents from 1305–1306 are cited in full in Ferdinando Neri, *I sonetti di Folgore da San Gimignano* (Città del Castello: Lapi, 1914): 13–15.

[4] Nicolino Applauso, "Folgore da San Gimignano e la parodia di Cenne: intrighi politici e poetici," in *La poesia italiana prima di Dante*, ed., Franco Suitner (Ravenna: Longo editore, 2017): 237–55, at 241–42.

[5] Philip Jones, *The Italian City-State: From Commune to Signoria* (Oxford: Clarendon Press, 1997): 152–55.

[6] Jones, *The Italian City-State*, 207–8.

historically inaccurate to speak of the urban nobility per se because marriages of expedience led to the blending of bloodlines;[7] the laws at the time do not mention aristocrats, but magnates, powerful and wealthy families irrespective of their lineages.[8] Yet the mindset of the cities remained feudal, as the ethos of nobility did not keep pace with the socio-economic developments.[9] As a reaction against all the changes in society, Folgore invoked the mythology of the courtly aristocracy of the Middle Ages. His writings about the nobility are not an exercise in mere nostalgia but stand in contrast to the degeneracy of his age. He satirically highlighted his dissatisfaction by depicting the courtly life, behaviors, and attitudes of a time gone by. In his poetry, he acknowledges that courtliness had waning relevance in his society but he possessed no other mental framework from which to conceptualize ethics and manners. The culture had not yet developed an ideological model for the new social realities of the Italian communes.

Folgore was not alone in clinging to the past—many individuals consciously presented themselves as the noble heroes of legend. Non-nobles adopted the trappings of nobility in public, wearing silver spurs or having their horses shod in precious metals.[10] Throughout the thirteenth century, an increasing number of parents named their children not after Christian saints but after the paladins of Charlemagne and the knights of the Round Table.[11] Readers of Dante's *Inferno* will recall his indignation at a Sienese "company of spendthrifts" (*brigata spendereccia*), who cast themselves in the roles of ancient noblemen.[12] In canto 13, and again in canto 29, Dante decries the immoderate spending of one such band of young men who strove to outdo each other in opulence. The fourteenth-century commentators of the *Comedy* speak of the company's feasts served on gold plates that were then ceremoniously tossed out the window, or foods cooked in exotic spices such as cloves or carnation leaves; they also mention the guests being served fried florins.[13] Benvenuto da Imola offers the sobering assessment

---

[7] Philip Jones, "Economia e società nell'Italia medievale: la leggenda della borghesia," in *Storia d'Italia: Annali*, vol. 1, *Dal feudalismo al capitalismo*, ed., Giulio Einaudi (Torino: Einaudi, 1978): 185–372, at 196.

[8] Carol Lansing, *The Florentine Magnates: Lineage and Faction in a Medieval Commune* (Princeton: Princeton University Press, 1991): 13–16.

[9] Franco Cardini, "Intellectuals and Culture in Twelfth- and Thirteenth-century Italy," in *City and Countryside in Late Medieval and Renaissance Italy: Essays Presented to Philip Jones*, eds., Trevor Dean and Chris Wickham (London and Ronceverte: The Hambledon Press, 1990): 13–30 (19).

[10] Jones, *The Italian City-State*, 313.

[11] Lansing, *The Florentine Magnates*, 156.

[12] Lansing, *The Florentine Magnates*, 161.

[13] Eugenio Ragni, "Brigata spendereccia," in *Enciclopedia Dantesca*, vol. 1 (Roma: Istituto della Enciclopedia Italiana, 1970): 699–700. See also Bartolomeo Aquarone, "Inferno XIII, XXIX," in *Dante in Siena ovvero accenni nella Divina Commedia a cose sanesi* (Città di Castello: Lapi, 1889): 27–46.

that in two short years the group spent the astronomical sum of 216,000 florins on such activities. The presence of bands of young men in Folgore's sonnet cycles led some to believe that Folgore praised the very same individuals that Dante condemned in *Inferno* 13 and 29. In fact, Benvenuto da Imola seemingly refers to Folgore's *corona* and Cenne's response in his discussion of *Inferno* 29: "Hence there have been written two pleasant songs about them; one of them contains their delights and pleasures, and the other the misfortunes and miseries they endured."[14] While it now seems highly unlikely that Folgore speaks of the same people as Dante, his poetry clearly reflects similar attitudes and practices.

In the cycle on the months, Folgore characterizes a group of individuals who have ostensibly formed their own "company of spendthrifts": Tengoccio, Min di Tengo, Ancaiano, Bartolo, Mugàvero, and Fainotto. Several of them are unknown, but Tengoccio may refer to Tengoccio di Baldo Grosso de' Tolomei (ca. 1323), Mugàvero may be Mogavero del Balza (ca. 1326), and perhaps Fainotto refers to Fainotto di Guido Squarcialupi (ca. 1320).[15] The leader of the group is Niccolò di Nisi, whom most scholars accept as Niccolò di Dionigi of San Gimignano (ca. 1309), a member of the Salimbeni family.[16] All the biographical dates for these individuals suggest that Folgore composed his *corona* in the early years of the fourteenth century.

Throughout the *corona* of the months, Folgore underscores the importance of the aristocratic virtue of generosity. In the introductory sonnet, the protagonist of the work is called as courteous as Lancelot or the sons of King Priam. In so doing, Folgore establishes an implicit contrast between the economics of a feudal society, which expected *largesse* from the nobility, and his contemporary society, where the acquisition and retention of money was paramount. He illustrates how the economic and political situation of the Italian communes has changed but the aristocratic ideals have not. But the poet goes further, because the sonnets of the months are presented as if a series of gifts to those men, thus reinforcing the aristocratic ideal of generosity found in the text. Throughout the cycle, Folgore claims he will give them pleasant activities, joyful living, and good

---

14 Benvenuto da Imola writes: "unde factae sunt duae cantiones [. . .] placibiles de eis; quarum altera continent delicias et delectiones eorum; altera vera calamitates et miserias, quas habituri erant."

15 Maurizio Vitale, ed., *Rimatori comico-realistici del Due e Trecento* (Torino: UTET, 1956): 580.

16 Giulio Navone, ed., *Le rime di Folgore da San Geminiano e di Cene da la Chitarra d'Arezzo* (Bologna: Commissione per i testi di lingua, 1968): xlix-lxvi. Recently Ubaldo Morandi noted the problems with the identification of Folgore's Niccolò di Nisi with Niccolò di Dionigi of the Salimbeni family, and proposed instead a different individual, Niccolò di Nici (ca. 1290–1340), a member of the Tolomei family. See Folgore da San Gimignano, *I sonetti dei mesi ed i componenti la brigata in una cronaca perugina del Trecento*, ed., Ubaldo Morandi (Siena: Cantagalli, 1991): 15–16.

food; he will give them beautiful landscapes, exciting cities, pleasant weather, and the company of courteous noblewomen and obsequious servants. In short, Folgore not only exalts the generosity of his fictional characters and of his readers, but also as the poet he positions himself within the ideological framework of courtesy. He too is generous, he implicitly states, for he is making a present of these poems and their settings to his characters.

Perhaps more so than in his other works, the cycle of the months demonstrates Folgore's unique poetic style. The poet uses a concrete lexicon, listing types of wild game, fish, foods, warm clothing, bed sheets, and elegant settings.[17] At the same time, Folgore also employs a large number of indeterminate adjectives and adverbs.[18] The poet frequently mentions "many" or "always," or uses specific numbers such as "twelve" or "thirty" but with the meaning of "a great quantity." Furthermore, Folgore tends to leave verbs in the infinitive instead of conjugating them. For example, he states that his gifts to the young men are "to dance" or "to hunt." By using the verbal infinitive, their actions take on a timeless quality; to dance is an ever-present aspect of aristocratic life. Objects are portrayed with specificity, but the reader has no linguistic markers to determine their quantity; actions, too, are depicted, but without any reference as to when they occurred or even who performed them. Together, the concrete lexicon, indeterminate descriptions and verbal infinitives create a dream-like effect.[19]

In this *corona*, Folgore's style corresponds most closely to the subject matter. Literature and artwork about the months of the year was common during the Middle Ages, and Folgore's *corona* needs to be viewed by the light of that tradition.[20] In the writings about the months of the year, the cyclical nature of time becomes foregrounded; human behavior may change from month to month, but across the years it remains the same. Aristocrats always fish in March for instance—always have and always will. By portraying the group's actions each month, Folgore underscores that the behaviors of the traditional aristocracy are not subject to the passage of time. Medieval Italian literature had absorbed the Provençal genre of the *plazer*, a rhymed composition in which the poet enumerated pleasant activities and things, and Folgore's poetry should be seen in the

---

[17] Maurizio Vitale, *La lingua dei poeti realistico-giocosi del '200 e del '300* (Milano: La Goliardica, 1955).

[18] Giovanni Caravaggi, "Il *plazer* di Folgore e il *plazer* degli stilnovisti," in *Il giuoco della vita bella: Folgore da San Gimignano: studi e testi*, ed., Michelangelo Picone (San Gimignano: Città di San Gimignano, 1988): 13–23; see also Rosario Ferreri, "I *sonetti de' mesi* di Folgòre da San Gimignano," *Romance Notes* 19 (1979): 395–98.

[19] Natalino Sapegno, "Poesia realistica e borghese," in *Il Trecento* (Milano: Vallardi, 1973): 63–108, at 97.

[20] Mario Marti, "Il 'sogno' di Folgore e la 'realtà' di Cenne," 131.

light of that tradition.[21] Texts of the *plazer* genre sometimes devolve into mere lists,[22] and Folgore's poetry reflects that trait as well. Folgore presents a society engaged in continuous joyfulness,[23] a refined hedonism that speaks of youth and generous courtesy.[24] Hence, he implies the beauty and timelessness of the noble values despite the changes in society.

Much of what was said about Folgore's cycle of the months can be applied to his cycle of the week. Here too, he describes the idealized actions of the nobility; they woo young ladies, joust, eat sumptuous feasts, and hunt with hounds. In the opening sonnet of the *corona* of the days of the week, Folgore mentions a particular individual, Carlo di Guerra Cavicciuoli. Carlo was a Florentine soldier who assisted San Gimignano in the war against Volterra in 1308; thus, it looks like Folgore composed the cycle during or shortly after the Volterran campaign. Perhaps Folgore described the idealized nobility to give Carlo's real-world actions a literary and ideological resonance. The campaign against Volterra was not merely one example of numerous wars of the early fourteenth century, Folgore seems to say; instead, Carlo's presence in San Gimignano brought back the glory of the great courts of the past. As with the months of the year, Folgore stresses the present-day relevance of Carlo's attributes, which are spelled out in the opening sonnet of the cycle: wisdom, valor, and courtesy.

The extant version of Folgore's third *corona*, about the vesting of a young knight, appears to be defective. The *corona*'s rubric in the single manuscript source, Riccardiano 2795, anticipates seventeen sonnets, but only five sonnets were transcribed.[25] The *corona* follows the ritualized bathing and clothing of the aspiring knight, as he is attended by allegorical figures. Prowess undresses the young man and embraces him, and Humility bathes him, cleansing him of all filth. In the final sonnet of the cycle, Gaiety arrives accompanied by a crowd of people who fête the soldier with song and dance as he enters society as a knight. Folgore modeled the cycle on the poem "L'ordene du Chevalierie" by Hues de Tabarye.[26] By adapting the French poem into a *corona*, or sonnet cycle, a dis-

---

[21] Raymond Thompson Hill, "The Enueg and Plazer in Mediaeval French and Italian," *PMLA* 30: 1 (1915): 42–63, at 42.

[22] Hill, "The Enueg and Plazer," 42.

[23] Adolfo Bartoli, "La poesia giocosa e satirica in Toscana," in *Storia della letteratura italiana*, vol. 2 (Firenze: Sansoni, 1879): 249–74, at 261.

[24] Giovanni Caravaggi, "Il *plazer* di Folgore e il *plazer* degli stilnovisti," in *Il giuoco della vita bella: Folgore da San Gimignano: studi e testi*, ed., Michelangelo Picone (San Gimignano: Città di San Gimignano, 1988): 13–23, at 15.

[25] For an overview of the sonnet cycle and its manuscripts, see Maria Pont, "Sonetti per l'armamento di un cavaliere," in *Il giuoco della vita bella: Folgore da San Gimignano: studi e testi*, ed., Michelangelo Picone (San Gimignano: Città di San Gimignano, 1988): 51–63.

[26] Caravaggi, *Folgore da S. Gimignano,* 156.

tinctly Italian form invented by Guittone d'Arezzo (ca. 1235/1294), he makes the statement that the martial virtues promoted by Hues de Tabarye are still pertinent in the age of the Italian communes. They are not merely motifs from literature of past centuries, but ideals to which contemporary soldiers, if not individuals throughout society, should aspire.

In addition to his three *corone*, Folgore wrote four sonnets about the wars in Tuscany during the second decade of the fourteenth century. His political sonnets are not part of larger collections, but are freestanding works about the threats that Pisa posed to its neighbors. Pisa was traditionally a stronghold of the Ghibellines, the party that allied itself with the Holy Roman Emperor in his struggle against the Pope and his followers, the Guelphs.[27] Folgore's city of San Gimignano, in contrast, was part of a league of Guelph communes that also included Florence and Lucca. In 1313, Uguccione della Faggiuola came to power in Pisa and declared war against the neighboring city of Lucca, eventually sacking that city. On 14 June 1314, Uguccione's army again entered Lucca and seized the treasure in the Cathedral of San Frediano. At the time, the political leader of the Guelphs in Italy was King Roberto II of Naples, a member of the French Angevin family. Despite Lucca's calls for assistance during the war with Pisa, King Roberto's aid at the time was negligible. A year later, on 29 August 1315, notwithstanding their greater numbers the combined Guelph forces of Naples and Florence were routed by Uguccione at the battle of Montecatini.

In his political sonnets Folgore insults the Pisan leaders and their Ghibelline followers, and chastises his fellow Guelphs for their cowardice and lack of military prowess. In contrast to his other poetry, Folgore uses an acerbic style in his political lyrics. He engages in *vituperium*, the poetics of insult, as he denigrates his intended readers.[28] It is in these sonnets that Folgore demonstrates indebtedness to the Florentine poet Rustico Filippi (ca. 1230/ca. 1299), who pioneered comic-satiric verse in the vernacular.[29] Like Filippi, Folgore heightens his satiric tone by writing second-person poetry, directly addressing the objects of his ire. He calls his enemies weaklings whose armor gives them a fearful appearance, and he accuses them of being as brave as rabbits, punning on the symbol of Pisa, the Hare. Folgore composes two sonnets against the members of his own party, the Guelphs, arguing that their fear has turned weak rabbits into lions, powerless owls into falcons. He advises the Guelphs that they should not hope for help from King Roberto II of Naples, explaining that the pious Roberto is too concerned with prayer, and thus has already made peace with Pisa; the King is not

[27] The historical background to the sonnets is culled from Carmelo Cappuccio, *Folgore da San Gimignano e Cene da la Chitarra* (Siracusa: Santoro, 1924): 80–81.

[28] Mario Marti, "Europeismo dell'antica letteratura giocosa," in *Cultura e stile nei poeti giocosi del tempo di Dante* (Pisa: Nistri-Lischi, 1953): 1–40, at 11–13.

[29] Fabian Alfie, "The Morality of Misogyny: The Case of Rustico Filippi, Vituperator of Women," *Quidditas* 25 (2004): 43–70, at 48–49.

concerned with those who have already died and whose bodies now serve as food for the wolves.

Additionally, Folgore tries to incite the Guelphs by recalling their lost kinsmen at the battle of Montecatini. In yet another second-person sonnet Folgore castigates God Himself for allowing events to turn against His party, the Guelphs. Folgore claims that he will not praise, serve, pray, or thank God, and notes that if Uguccione requested a toll, Christ would pay it without hesitation; the latter assertion appears to refer to the despoiling of the Lucchese Cathedral of San Frediano. In his political sonnets, Folgore clearly alludes to the struggles between the Ghibellines and the Guelphs, and therefore all four of his political poems can be dated between 1313 and 1317. Thanks to the style adopted in his political sonnets, Folgore is categorized among the comic-realistic poets of the Middle Ages (*poesia giocosa*).[30] Yet despite their stylistic and tonal differences from the three *corone*, Folgore's political poems are not atypical for him. All his poetry, rather, is engaged in the political, social, and moral crises afflicting the society of the Italian comunes.

Folgore also composed a sonnet about the loss of courtly behavior in contemporary society; "I call," he writes, "Courtesy, courtesy, courtesy." With its explicit reference to courtly ideals, this sonnet clearly encapsulates Folgore's social ideology.[31] Despite his calls for people to be courteous, no one answers him. Instead, greed holds sway over the population and destroys all virtue. The reference to greed seems to be a veiled allusion to the mercantile ethos of the age, which is contrasted to the noble liberality of the past. Three additional sonnets may have been written by Folgore, although their attribution is uncertain. In them, the poet sententiously promotes ethical living; he warns against letting desires overrule a person's intellect, cautions against judging from mere appearances, and explains how the system of noble virtues is derived from virtue. In these sonnets, too, he levels an implicit critique of contemporary society by exhorting his readers to return to the manners of the past.

The names of Folgore da San Gimignano and Cenne da la Chitarra are bound to one another. Little is known about Cenne da la Chitarra. In the earliest archival document of his life, dated 1322, Cenne is referred to as still living ("presentibus Cenne olim [. . .] qui dicitur alias Cenne da la Chitarra").[32] Nicolino Applauso has recently unearthed a document indicating the date of Cenne's death as 1334.[33] The final document, dated 1336, enumerates his surviving heirs

[30] Caravaggi, *Folgore da S. Gimignano*, 20.

[31] Claude Perrus, "Courtoisie et décadence dans la poésie de Folgore da San Gimignano," *Revue des études italiennes* 9 (1962): 5–32, at 6.

[32] The archival document is cited in Carmelo Cappuccio, *Folgore da S. Gemignano e Cene da la Chitarra* (Siracusa: Santoro, 1924): 13.

[33] Applauso, "Folgore da San Gimignano e la parodia di Cenne: intrighi politici e poetici," 246.

("[. . .] unam domum positam Aretii in populo Sancti Bartholomei iuxta heredis Cennis da la Chitarra").[34] The guitar of his nickname suggests that he was a professional jongleur, since jongleurs were frequently known by their musical instruments. Everything else about Cenne's life remains a mystery.

Cenne's poetic production consists of thirteen sonnets, which are a line-by-line parody of Folgore's *corona* of the months. Cenne's *corona* is comprised of sonnets about the twelve months plus one introductory sonnet, but not a concluding sonnet as in Folgore's composition. Where Folgore had composed a *plazer*, Cenne offers an *enueg*, the genre counterpoised to the *plazer* in which the poet lists annoyances and vexations.[35] Cenne utilizes the common technique of responding *per le rime*, that is, of using the same rhymes as those found in Folgore's cycle. Throughout the months, he replaces Folgore's warm fireplaces with smoky ones; his group must sleep in uncomfortable beds, suffer bitter winter winds, endure poverty, and drink soured wines. At times Cenne imitates the very phrases used by Folgore, but upturns them by presenting ugliness instead. Cenne's is a complete reaction to Folgore's *corona* of the months that recasts Folgore's idealized settings with negative ones.

Yet Cenne may not have simply been a nay-sayer to Folgore's rosy world. In his *corona* Cenne overturns the very values expressed by Folgore. In the opening sonnet, Cenne imagines a greedy group of young men gambling with dice and then wandering off in their undershirts when they lose. In so doing, Cenne evokes the medieval ideology of the tavern in his sonnet. As a concept, the tavern was the locus of all that was negative in the world, a type of symbolic anti-church where one drank, diced, caroused with prostitutes, and awoke the next morning atop a dunghill, robbed and stripped bare.[36] Across numerous texts throughout the Middle Ages, the tavern was the standard literary convention for the depiction of irreligious practices and for comic impiety.[37] Additionally, in place of Folgore's emphasis on courtesy Cenne stresses poverty (e.g., sonnet 12, v. 3), and avariciousness (e.g., sonnet 8, v. 13). Cenne's depiction of the peasantry and of old, homely women denoted the ideological opposite of medieval courtliness. Peasants, the social counterpoint to the aristocracy, were routinely described during the Middle Ages as ugly: crudely formed, coarse-featured, and dark-skinned.[38] At the end of his sonnet to September, Cenne claims that the

---

[34] The archival document is cited in Carmelo Cappuccio, *Folgore da S. Gemignano e Cene da la Chitarra*, 13.

[35] Raymond Thompson Hill, "The Enueg," *PMLA* 27: 2 (1912): 265–296, at 265.

[36] Andrew Cowell, *At Play in the Tavern: Signs, Coins and Bodies in the Middle Ages* (Ann Arbor: University of Michigan Press, 1999): 6–8.

[37] Martha Bayless, *Parody in the Middle Ages: The Latin Tradition* (Ann Arbor: University of Michigan Press, 1996): 94.

[38] Paul Freedman, *Images of the Medieval Peasant* (Stanford: Stanford University Press, 1999): 139–40.

Salimbeni family exiled the defenders of courtesy (vv. 13–14). Thus, like Folgore's, Cenne's *corona* may be viewed as a political satire, at least in part. Cenne's response may have been a partisan slander, because he insults the family exalted by Folgore in his cycle of months. Here, the Salimbeni are associated with the low-born, and distanced from the values of the nobility.

While Cenne da la Chitarra must be read side-by-side with Folgore da San Gimignano, the Lucchese poet Pietro dei Faitinelli nicknamed Il Mugnone (ca. 1285–90/1349) stands as a writer in his own right. Nonetheless, his verse shows the influence of Folgore, in particular when he decries the political situation in Tuscany. Pietro is the author of some sixteen sonnets, one *canzone*, and one *frottola*, of which eleven sonnets deal with the political turmoil afflicting Lucca. Like Folgore, Pietro dei Faitinelli complains about the Pisan lord Uguccione della Faggiuola and of the insufficient help from Roberto II, but he also vituperates Uguccione's Lucchese general, Castruccio Castracani (1281–1328). A member of the Antinelli family, Castruccio acted as a mercenary for Uguccione in the war against Lucca in 1314 and at the battle of Montecatini in 1315.[39] Later in the decade, Uguccione turned against Castruccio and had him jailed, but Castruccio was freed when he led an insurrection. Castruccio took power over Lucca and his success led to decades of Ghibelline rule over the city.

As is the case with many writers of the Italian Middle Ages, the biographical facts about Pietro dei Faitinelli are scant. The Faitinelli (spelled at the time as Faytinelli) were listed among the most powerful families of Lucca, the *potentes* and *casatici*, in 1308.[40] The date of Pietro's birth is unknown, but in 1315 he numbered among the mounted soldiers from Sesto San Piero Scheraggio in the battle of Montecatini who were taken prisoner by the Pisan forces. Thus, the date of his birth can be extrapolated to ca. 1285–1290. After seventeen years of exile, during which he probably took refuge in the Veneto, he returned to the Lucca on 12 August 1331. For eighteen years, he worked as a notary until his death on 23 November 1349.[41]

One biographical anecdote about Pietro has thus far escaped the attention of literary scholars. Although apocryphal, it offers a glimpse of the man behind the poetry. Years before Pietro's birth, on 27 April 1278, one of the servants in Faitinelli household, Zita, passed away. The daughter of poor farmers in Monsagrati, Zita was born around 1210, and at twelve years of age she was indentured to the Faitinelli family. At first the family treated her cruelly, but over time her

[39] Information about Castruccio Castracani is culled from Christine Meek, *The Commune of Lucca under Pisan Rule, 1342–1369* (Cambridge, MA: The Medieval Academy of America, 1980): 1.

[40] Christine Meek, *Lucca 1369–1400. Politics and Society in an Early Renaissance City-State* (Oxford: Oxford University Press, 1978): 190.

[41] The biographical data about Pietro dei Faitinelli are culled from Leone Del Prete, *Rime di Ser Pietro dei Faytinelli* (Bologna: Romagnoli, 1874): 23–43.

devotion to God had softened them to her.[42] She turned the family to God, and news of her ministry spread throughout Lucca. She offered her bed to shelter pilgrims and prostitutes, and despite her meager wages she gave liberally to the destitute.[43] Four years after her death, the Bishop of Lucca authorized the cult venerating her memory, and by the early fourteenth century, Zita's name was indissolubly linked to the city of Lucca.[44] Fazio degli Uberti uses the name Saint Zita to designate the Commune (3:6), and Dante refers to one of its political leaders as the "Elders of Saint Zita" (*Inferno* 21: 38). But she was officially canonized by the Catholic Church centuries later.

The anecdote about Pietro dei Faitinelli appears in the earliest biography of Saint Zita contained in the fourteenth-century manuscript owned by the Faitinelli family. During a trip to Provence, Pietro fell gravely ill. Three doctors were summoned, and they all concurred that he was dying. With all his heart, he called on the soul of Zita to help him, and during the night she appeared to him in a vision. She told him not to fear, and she healed him by placing her hands upon him. The next morning he awoke healthy, and he requested food from his servant. The servant wondered who had visited Pietro because, she said, during the night she had heard Pietro conversing with someone (Chapter 5: 38).[45] This

42 Niccolò Del Re, "Zita," in *Bibliotheca Sanctorum*, vol. 12 (Roma: Istituto Giovanni XXIII della Pontificia Università Lateranense, 1969): 1484.

43 Michael Goodich, "*Ancilla Dei*: The Servant as Saint in the Late Middle Ages," in *Women of the Medieval World*, ed., Julius Kirshner and Suzanne F. Wempel (Oxford: Blackwell, 1985): 119–36, at 128.

44 Niccolò Del Re, "Zita," 1484.

45 The Chapter reads: "Intra defunctionis hujus ancillae Dei quidam juvenis, videlicet Petrus de Faytinellis, qui eadem in domo Faytinellorum de Luca fuerat enutritus, dum per provinciam Provinciae iter faceret, in gravissimam incidit infirmitatem: [cuidam a Medicis deposito,] quae adeo ipsum affligendo momordit, ut tres famosi medici, qui curationi ejus studiose intendebant, de ipsius tandem convalescentia desperati, concorditer eumdem in crastinum moriturum firmiter ad invicem asseruerunt. Quod dum ille aeger intellexisset, tota mente invocavit B. Zitam, dulci & familiari alloquio, veluti facere puerulus consueverat; inter alia conquerendo, quod cum abesset a propriis, nec paternum aut maternum vel aliorum suorum sibi adesset subsidium vel consilium, non permitteret abesse juvamen. Et ecce nocte sequenti, nec dormienti nec plene vigilanti, apparuit coram eo Veneranda Zita, [apparens in Gallia,] in veste serica, quam varia & artificiosa textura opificis admirabilem exhibebat, coronam eminentem in capite gestans, grossis & preciosibus lapidibus decoratam: sed vultum vetustatis suae, qualem vivens in corpore gerebat, ut a dicto juvene Petro indubitanter agnosceretur, videbatur habere: quam quidem Zitam duo lumina facularum vel cereorum splendida praecedebant. Et licet luminum portitores idem Petrus non videret, eam tamen plenius videns, citius recognovit: ad quam taliter est affatus: O Domina mea Zita, subvenite mihi, qui taliter sum destitutus & afflictus, nec est aliquis ex nostris qui mihi opem valet afferre. At illa inquit: Noli timere. Et iterum inquit ille: Quis est vobiscum? Illa vero respondit: [sanitatem restituit,] Tace noli tantum quaerere; constans esto. Extendensque protinus manum apposuit eam fronti juvenis

anecdote is an important reminder of Pietro's place, and that of his family, in Lucchese history.

The narrative about Saint Zita not only sheds light on Pietro's biography, but may also affect how one reads his poetry. Faitinelli left one *canzone*, a multi-stanza poem that treats a matter of high importance. In "Courtesy is dead, *largesse* is dead," which consists of five stanzas, Pietro inveighs against the corrupt state of contemporary society. The opening strophe deals with the loss of courtly values, such as courtesy, *largesse*, gentleness, honor, and loyalty; these values have been destroyed by impiety, betrayals, and greed. The social critique of the first stanza echoes much of what Folgore had written about the loss of noble virtues in his sonnet, "I call 'Courtesy, courtesy, courtesy.'" Pietro's second strophe elaborates on the first, as he describes the backward standards of contemporary society; nowadays, he writes, rich fools are considered wise, loyal service is disregarded, and bloodlines, brotherhood, and love of party are worthless. The loss of traditional values is not merely a social ill, he writes in the third stanza, because the Christian ideals of neighborly love, rejection of vice, and teachings of virtue are also gone. It is in this stanza, more than anywhere else, that Pietro's adherence to Christian teachings comes to the fore. However, the trope of *contemptus mundi*, the satire of the fallen world and perverse society that have strayed from Christian beliefs, was an ancient Christian subject matter revitalized after the first millennium by writers such as Peter Damian (1007–1072), Hermann Contract (1013–1054), Roger of Caen (d. 1139), Bernard of Cluny (twelfth century), and it was developed fully by Pope Innocent III (1160–1216); it remained a topic of religious writers for centuries afterward.[46] Like other authors of *contemptus mundi,* Pietro expresses regret over the loss of virtue, and rage over the current situation.[47] Thus, while Pietro makes no explicit mention of his family's exalted servant, her Christian teachings are not foreign to his writings.

Though Pietro writes about the changing social mores in his *canzone*, the majority of his poetic corpus deals with the political strife afflicting Lucca, and

aegrotantis, & ipsum sanavit continuo, statimque ab oculis ejus evanuit. Surrexit igitur sanus, & inquit ad ministram suam: Affer mihi manducare, quia sanus sum. At illa dixit: O fili, requiesce, ut sanus esses: dicito quoque mihi cum quibus modo loquebaris? audivi enim te loquentem & aliam personam respondentem, cum qua sermocinabaris. Juvenis quoque rei seriem totam aperuit, adjecitque, prius ipse videret & sciret illos tres medicos morituros, qui ipsum prognosticabantur ad mortem, quam moreretur ipse. Quod & vere post non multum tempus evenit." Cited from *Acta Sanctorum quotquot toto orbe coluntur, vel a catholicis scriptoribus celebrantur*, vol. 12, eds. Godifrido Henschenio and Daniele Papebrochio (Paris and Rome: Bibliopolam, 1866): 514.

46 Jean Delumeau, *Sin and Fear: The Emergence of a Western Guilt Culture, 13th-18th Centuries*, trans., Eric Nicholson (New York: St. Martin's Press, 1990): 9–22.

47 Ronald E. Pepin, *Scorn for the World: Bernard of Cluny's* De contemptu mundi. *The Latin Text with English Translation and an Introduction* (East Lansing: Medieval Texts and Studies, 1991): xii.

the eleven sonnets on political topics best illustrate Folgore's influence on him. Like Folgore, he criticizes King Roberto II, the leader of the Italian Guelphs, calling him Charles I's heir, but not the inheritor of Charles's valor; Pietro anticipates that Roberto's equivocation will allow the Ghibellines to despoil him of his lands. Elsewhere, he incites his fellow Guelphs to battle, and urges whoever captures Uguccione not to kill him but to lead him to a Florentine prison. Like Folgore, Pietro chides the Guelphs in several sonnets for their weakness and ineffective strategy. He warns the Guelphs not to be distracted by their ostentation and earnings, but to focus on warfare; they will need to loosen their purse strings if they want to defeat Uguccione and his Pisan Ghibellines, Faitinelli writes. He also decries the Pisan victories, describing himself as castrated by Castruccio and wondering aloud where he will find joy now that Lucca has been subjugated. He fears that Uguccione will become the lord of all of Tuscany if the Guelphs do not succeed at reining him in, and he envisions the destruction that would ensue. Together, Folgore and Pietro depict the frustration, dismay, and fear of the Guelphs of Western Tuscany in the early *Trecento.*

Yet Pietro's political poetry is not merely about partisan concerns. Rather, he frequently views the social corruption as a broader concern. In one sonnet, he writes that Christ always puts an end to pride and egotism, and as proof of this he lists the Sicilian rebellion against Charles I, commonly known as the Sicilian Vespers, and the overthrow of the lords of Milan, the Torriani, by the Visconti. In his *frottola,* a lengthy poem of irregular stanzas typically used for satires, he writes about the situation in Lucca. He lists off various citizens, noting how the Lucchese magnates have debased themselves by becoming shopkeepers, merchants, blacksmiths, and street sweepers. He ironically concludes that Castruccio has put an end to their infighting. But one sonnet in particular explicitly demonstrates Pietro dei Faitinelli's indebtedness to Folgore da San Gimignano. Much as Folgore had blamed God for the Guelphs' defeats, resulting in his determination to withhold his adoration of Him, so too is Pietro determined to punish Christ. Faitinelli writes that he would rather venerate Apollo, Vesta, Hercules, or Minerva, or convert to Judaism or Islam, rather than continue to follow Jesus; the reason, he explains, is that God allows evil men to thrive while the just are laid low.[48] Faitinelli transforms Folgore's distinctly political statement into one of social criticism. Lastly, he writes about the pain of exile, imagining that the great joy he will feel when he returns to Lucca will cause him to embrace even his enemies; this sonnet is based on a similar one by the Sienese poet Cecco

[48] For a thorough examination of the relationship between these two sonnets, along with others like them, see Fabian Alfie, "Punishing God: Politically Motivated Blasphemy in the Italian Comic Poetry of the Fourteenth Century," *Medievalia et Humanistica* 30 (2003): 33–54.

Angiolieri (ca. 1260/1312), and it influenced another sonnet by the Florentine Pieraccio Tedaldi (ca. 1285–90/ca. 1350).[49]

Pietro dei Faitinelli also composes sonnets based on traditional motifs. He writes two misogynistic poems, explaining that men can understand science, theology, and alchemy, but they can never understand women because they are so deceitful. Indeed, he explains in another poem, women are so evil that the only women allowed into Heaven are given access simply to keep company with the Virgin Mary. In another sonnet, he complains about his wife, calling on Death to carry her off. The subject matter of misogyny was a part of the comic-satiric tradition that had a dual set of roots: in the classical satires of Juvenal, Ovid and Sallust, and later, in the teachings of the Church Fathers.[50] Saints Jerome, Augustine, and others borrowed tropes from classical satirists about women's faults originally with the purpose of enforcing monastic chastity.[51] The presence of misogynistic material in the fourteenth-century Italian poetry reflects the strong impact that such teachings still had on medieval culture. It may also have served a secondary function, however, as a type of *sic et non* reasoning introduced into the literary culture, counterpoising a negative portrayal of women to the exaltation of women in love literature. These various strains of cultural, literary, and religious thought inform the sonnets in Pietro's corpus. And in another poem altogether, Pietro offers the sententious advice that the readers not be taken in by other people's appearances.

Sources and Translations:

The most important manuscript for Folgore da San Gimignano is Vatican Barberiniano Latin 3953, which contains twenty-nine sonnets and includes the *corone* of the days of the week and the months of the year. The *corona* of the months, in less complete forms, appears in five other codices.[52] The *corona* of the prepara-

[49] For a thorough examination of the three sonnets about exile, see Fabian Alfie, "Cast Out: The Topos of Exile in Cecco Angiolieri, Pietro de' Faitinelli and Pieraccio Tedaldi," *Annali d'Italianistica* 20 (2002): 113–24.

[50] See P. G. Walsh, "Antifeminism in the High Middle Ages," in *Satiric Advice on Women and Marriage: From Plautus to Chaucer*, ed., Warren S. Smith (Ann Arbor: The University of Michigan Press, 2005): 222–42, at 224–25. See also Ralph Hanna III and Traugott Lawler, eds., *Jankyn's Book of Wikked Wives: The Primary Texts*, vol. 1 (Athens & London: Georgia University Press, 1997), 18.

[51] Katharina M. Wilson and Elizabeth M. Makowski, *Wykked Wyves and the Woes of Marriage: Misogamous Literature from Juvenal to Chaucer* (Albany: State University of New York Press, 1990): 1.

[52] The five other manuscripts containing Folgore's *corona* of the months are: Magliabechiano VII 1066 at the Central Library of Florence; MS 1158 of the Riccardiana Library of Florence; Chigiano L. IV. 131 of the Apostolic Library of the Vatican; a

tion of the knight is only found in manuscript 2795 of the Riccardiana Library of Florence. Cenne da la Chitarra's poems are found only in the Vatican Barberiniano Latin 3953 codex. Scholars typically use the readings of Folgore da San Gimignano, Cenne da la Chitarra, and Pietro dei Faitinelli from Mario Marti's anthology of medieval comic poetry;[53] also reliable are the anthologies by Maurizio Vitale and by Aldo Francesco Massèra.[54] In this volume, unless otherwise noted, Mario Marti's readings are the basis for all the transcriptions, with other scholars' variants listed in the footnotes. One other edition warrants comment: in 1969 Pietro di Sano illustrated the sonnets of months as if transcribed into an illuminated manuscript.[55] The codicological tradition for Pietro dei Faitinelli presents a distinct challenge, as it is divided between codices produced in Tuscany, and those that originated in the Veneto.[56] The *lectiones* published by Leone del Prete and Anna Paola Zilli reproduce two sets of poems, each reflecting the local dialects of the manuscripts.[57]

To date, the poems of Folgore da San Gimignano and the responses by Cenne da la Chitarra have not been translated into English in their entirety. The most thorough was Dante Gabriel Rossetti, who in 1861 translated two of Folgore's political poems (sonnets 30 and 31), a moralizing sonnet of questioned

---

codex of the Seminario of Fermo, and a privately owned manuscript from Perugia. For an overview of the manuscript tradition, see Anna Bettarini Bruni, "Osservazioni sulla tradizione manoscritta di Folgore da San Gimignano," in *Il giuoco della vita bella: Folgore da San Gimignano: studi e testi*, ed., Michelangelo Picone (San Gimignano: Città di San Gimignano, 1988): 65–78. See also Folgore da San Gimignano, *I sonetti dei mesi ed i componenti la brigata in una cronaca perugina del Trecento*, ed., Ubaldo Morandi.

[53] Mario Marti, ed., *I poeti giocosi del tempo di Dante* (Milano: Rizzoli, 1956).

[54] Maurizio Vitale, ed., *Rimatori comico-realistici del Due e Trecento* (Torino: UTET, 1956); and Aldo Francesco Massèra, ed., *Sonetti burleschi e realistici dei primi due secoli* (Bari: Laterza, 1940).

[55] Folgore da San Gimignano, *I mesi di Folgore da San Gimignano illustrati da Sano di Pietro* (Roma: Banca Nazionale dell'Agricoltura, 1969).

[56] The most important manuscript for Pietro dei Faitinelli's poetry is Vatican Barberiniano Latin 3953. The others are as follows: from the Laurentian Library in Florence, MS 15, Gaddiano 198, Reddiano 184; from the Riccardiana Library in Florence, MSS 1003, 1088, and 1156; from the Central Library of Florence, MSS II ii 40, and Magliabechiano VII 1034; from the Marucelliana Library in Florence, MS C 155; from the Trivulziano Library in Milan, 36; and from Lucca, Moück 1 and 77. For an overview of Pietro's manuscript tradition, see Leone del Prete, ed, *Rime di Ser Pietro dei Faytinelli* (Bologna: Romagnoli, 1874): 66. See also Benedetta Aldinucci, "Il notaio Pietro de' Faitinelli da Lucca, detto Mugnone: Nuove proposte per l'edizione delle Rime," in *I cantieri dell'italianistica. Ricerca, didattica e organizzazione agli inizi del XXI secolo* (Roma: Adi editore, 2014): 1–11; and Fabian Alfie, "Noterella sulle rime di Pietro de' Faitinelli: Il Magliabechiano VII 1034," *Letteratura Italiana Antica* 8 (2007): 137–40.

[57] Leone Del Prete, *Rime di Ser Pietro dei Faytinelli*, and Anna Paola Zilli, "Le rime di Pietro de' Faitinelli," *Quaderni lucchesi* 1:1 (gennaio-giugno 2000): 11–104.

attribution (sonnet 35), the complete *corone* of the months, and of the days of the week.[58] In 1945, Richard Aldington published *A Wreath for San Gemignano*, a volume dedicated exclusively to Folgore's fourteen sonnets of the months in English, illustrated by Netta Aldington.[59] Fifteen years later, Thomas Caldecott Chubb published Folgore's twelve sonnets of the months in a facing-page translation, which also included woodcut prints from a Venetian edition of the *Decameron* from 1518.[60] Chubb did not include the opening and closing sonnets of the cycle, however. In his anthology of medieval Italian poetry, Joseph Tusiani rendered Folgore's twelve sonnets of the months into English; like Chubb he omitted the introductory or concluding sonnets to the *corona*, yet unlike the others he included four of Cenne's months as well (January, February, May, and June).[61] Pietro dei Faitinelli has never been translated into English. This volume constitutes the first time that the complete poetry of the three poets has been available to readership in English. In my translations, I have tried to keep the meter of the original sonnets whenever possible, but not the rhymes. Since the poets mention historical persons and events, I have added clarifying comments before many of the poems, and I have added footnotes to clarify the language. Throughout, I have strived to render the medieval Italian in accurate, readable English, making the poems as accessible as possible to contemporary readers.

[58] Dante Gabriel Rossetti, *The Early Italian Poets From Ciullo D'Alcamo to Dante Alighieri (1100–1200–1300)* (London: Smith, Elder, and Co., 1861): 330–45. Rossetti's sonnets of the months are reprinted with illustrations in *Of the Months: Twelve Sonnets Addressed to Fellowship of Sienese Nobles by Folgore da San Geminiano*, trans., Dante Gabriel Rossetti (Northwood: Knights Press [n.d.]).

[59] Richard Aldington, *A Wreath for San Gemignano* (New York: Duell, Sloan and Pearce, Inc., 1945).

[60] Thomas Caldecott Chubb, *The Months of the Year: Twelve Sonnets by Folgore da San Gimignano* (Sanbornville, NH: Wake-Brook House, 1960).

[61] Joseph Tusiani, *The Age of Dante: An Anthology of Early Italian Poetry* (New York: Baroque Press, 1974): 40–49.

Bibliography

Aldington, Richard. *A Wreath for San Gemignano.* New York: Duell, Sloan and Pearce, Inc., 1945.

Aldinucci, Benedetta. "Il notaio Pietro de' Faitinelli da Lucca, detto Mugnone: Nuove proposte per l'edizione delle Rime." In *I cantieri dell'italianistica. Ricerca, didattica, e organizzazione agli inizi del XXI secolo.* Edited by B. Alfonzetti, G. Baldassari, and F. Tomasi. Roma: Adi Editore, 2014. 1–11.

Alfie, Fabian. "Cast Out: The Topos of Exile in Cecco Angiolieri, Pietro de' Faitinelli and Pieraccio Tedaldi." *Annali d'Italianistica* 20 (2002): 113–24.

———. "The Morality of Misogyny: The Case of Rustico Filippi, Vituperator of Women." *Quidditas* 25 (2004): 43–70.

———. "Noterella sulle rime di Pietro de' Faitinelli: Il Magliabechiano VII 1034." *Letteratura Italiana Antica* 8 (2007): 137–40.

———. "Punishing God: Politically Motivated Blasphemy in the Italian Comic Poetry of the Fourteenth Century." *Medievalia et Humanistica* 30 (2003): 33–54.

Alighieri, Dante. *The Divine Comedy of Dante Alighieri*, vol. 1, *Inferno.* Edited and translated by Robert M. Durling, with introduction and notes by Ronald L. Martinez and Robert M. Durling. New York, Oxford: Oxford University Press, 1996.

Apollonio, Mario. "La realtà nuova e Folgore." In *Uomini e forme nella cultura italiana delle origini.* Firenze: Sansoni, 1943. 282–301.

Applauso, Nicolino. "Folgore da San Gimignano e la parodia di Cenne: intrighi politici e poetici." In *La poesia italiana prima di Dante.* Edited by Franco Suitner. Ravenna: Longo Editore, 2017. 237–55.

Aquarone, Bartolomeo. "Inferno—XIII, XXIX." In *Dante in Siena ovvero accenni nella Divina Commedia a cose sanesi.* Città del Castello: Lapi, 1889. 27–46.

Bartoli, Adolfo. "La poesia giocosa e satirica in Toscana." In *Storia della letteratura italiana*, vol. 2. Firenze: Sansoni, 1879. 249–74.

Bayless, Martha. *Parody in the Middle Ages: The Latin Tradition.* Ann Arbor, The University of Michigan Press, 1996.

Borgognoni, Adolfo. "Bindo Bonichi e alcuni altri rimatori senesi." In *Studi d'erudizione e d'arte*, vol. 1. Bologna: Romagnoli, 1877–1878. 1–119.

Brambilla Ageno, Franca. "Per l'interpretazione di Cenne della Chitarra." *Studi medievali* 7: 1 (1966): 197–201.

Bruni, Anna Bettarini. "Osservazioni sulla tradizione manoscritta di Folgore da San Gimignano." In *Il giuoco della vita bella: Folgore da San Gimignano: studi e testi.* Edited by Michelangelo Picone. San Gimignano: Città di San Gimignano, 1988. 65–78.

Cappuccio, Carmelo. *Folgore da San Gimignano e Cene da la Chitarra.* Siracusa: Santoro, 1924.

Caravaggi, Giovanni. *Folgore da S. Gimignano*. Milano: Ceschina, 1960.

———. "Il *plazer* di Folgore e il *plazer* degli stilnovisti." In *Il giuoco della vita bella: Folgore da San Gimignano: studi e testi*. Edited by Michelangelo Picone. San Gimignano: Città di San Gimignano, 1988. 13–23.

Cardini, Franco. "Intellectuals and Culture in Twelfth- and Thirteenth-Century Italy." In *City and Countryside in Late Medieval and Renaissance Italy: Essays Presented to Philip Jones*. Edited by Trevor Dean and Chris Wickham. London and Ronceverte: The Hambledon Press, 1990. 13–30.

Carducci, Giosuè. *Studi intorno ad alcune rime del secolo XIII e XIV.* Imola: Galeati, 1876. 43–49.

Chubb, Thomas Caldecott. *The Months of the Year: Twelve Sonnets by Folgore da San Gimignano*. Sanbornville, NH: Wake-Brook House, 1960.

Cian, Vittorio. *La satira*. Vallardi: Milano, 1929. 135–47.

Ciccuto, Marcello. "Folgore laico." In *Il giuoco della vita bella: Folgore da San Gimignano: studi e testi*. Edited by Michelangelo Picone. San Gimignano: Città di San Gimignano, 1988. 41–50.

Cowell, Andrew. *At Play in the Tavern: Signs, Coins and Bodies in the Middle Ages*. Ann Arbor, University of Michigan Press, 1999.

Del Prete, Leone, ed. *Rime di Ser Pietro dei Faytinelli*. Bologna: Romagnoli, 1874.

Del Re, Niccolò. "Zita." In *Bibliotheca Sanctorum*, Vol. 12. Roma: Istituto Giovanni XXIII della Pontificia Università Lateranense, 1969. 1484.

Delumeau, Jean. *Sin and Fear: The Emergence of a Western Guilt Culture, 13th–18th Centuries*. Translated by Eric Nicholson. New York: St. Martin's Press, 1990.

Ferreri, Rosario. "I *sonetti de' mesi* di Folgòre da San Gimignano." *Romance Notes* 19 (1979): 395–98.

Folena, Gianfranco. Review of Ireneo Sanesi's article "Fòlgore o Folgòre?" *La rassegna della letteratura italiana* 67: 2 (Maggio-Settembre, 1963): 327–28.

Folgore da San Gimignano. *I mesi di Folgore da San Gimignano illustrati da Sano di Pietro*. Roma: Banca Nazionale dell'Agricoltura, 1969.

———. *Of the Months: Twelve Sonnets Addressed to Fellowship of Sienese Nobles by Folgore da San Geminiano*. Translated by Dante Gabriel Rossetti. Northwood: Knights Press [n.d.].

———. *I sonetti dei mesi ed i componenti la brigata in una cronaca perugina del Trecento*. Edited by Ubaldo Morandi. Siena: Cantagalli, 1991.

Freedman, Paul. *Images of the Medieval Peasant*. Stanford: Stanford University Press, 1999.

Goodich, Michael. "*Ancilla Dei*: The Servant as Saint in the Late Middle Ages." In *Women of the Medieval World*. Edited by Julius Kirshner and Suzanne F. Wempel. Oxford: Blackwell, 1985. 119–36.

Guerrieri Crocetti, Camillo. *La lirica predantesca*. Firenze: Vallecchi, 1925.

Hanna III, Ralph, and Traugott Lawler, eds. *Jankyn's Book of Wikked Wives: The Primary Texts*, vol. 1. Athens & London: Georgia University Press, 1997.

Henschenio, Godifrido, and Daniele Papebrochio, eds. *Acta Sanctorum quotquot toto orbe coluntur, vel a catholicis scriptoribus celebrantur*, vol. 12. Paris and Rome: Bibliopolam, 1866. 514.

Hill, Raymond Thompson. "The Enueg." *PMLA* 27: 2 (1912): 265–96.

———. "The Enueg and Plazer in Mediaeval French and Italian." *PMLA* 30: 1 (1915): 42–63.

Jones, Philip. "Economia e società nell'Italia medievale: La leggenda della borgesia." In *Storia d'Italia: Annali*, vol. 1. *Dal feudalismo al capitalismo.* Edited by Giulio Einaudi. Torino: Einaudi, 1978. 185–372.

———. *The Italian City-State: From Commune to Signoria.* Oxford: Clarendon Press, 1997.

Lansing, Carol. *The Florentine Magnates: Lineage and Faction in a Medieval Commune.* Princeton: Princeton University Press, 1991.

"Le due corone: sonetti della *semana* e dei *mesi* con il commento di Michelangelo Picone." In *Il giuoco della vita bella: Folgore da San Gimignano: studi e testi.* Edited by Michelangelo Picone. San Gimignano: Città di San Gimignano, 1988. 79–126.

Li Gotti, Ettore. "Cecco e Folgòre." In *Saggi.* Firenze: La Nuova Italia, 1941. 19–35.

Lombardi-Lotti, Mansueto. *La poesia politica di Pietro de' Faytinelli da Lucca.* Lucca: Nuova Grafica lucchese, 1972.

Marti, Mario. "Europeismo dell'antica letteratura giocosa." In *Cultura e stile nei poeti giocosi del tempo di Dante.* Pisa: Nistri-Lischi, 1953. 1–40.

———. "Pietro dei Faitinelli e le rime politiche dei poeti giocosi." In *Cultura e stile nei poeti giocosi del tempo di Dante.* Pisa: Nistri-Lischi, 1953. 153–69.

———, ed. *I poeti giocosi del tempo di Dante.* Milano: Rizzoli, 1956.

———. "Il 'sogno' di Folgore e la 'realtà' di Cenne." In *Cultura e stile dei poeti giocosi del tempo di Dante.* Pisa: Nistri-Lischi, 1953. 131–52.

Massèra, Aldo Francesco, ed. *Sonetti burleschi e realistici dei primi due secoli.* Bari: Laterza, 1940.

Meek, Christine. *The Commune of Lucca under Pisan Rule, 1342–1369.* Cambridge, MA: The Medieval Academy of America, 1980.

———. *Lucca 1369–1400. Politics and Society in an Early Renaissance City-State.* Oxford: Oxford University Press, 1978.

Morandi, Ubaldo, ed. *I sonetti dei mesi ed i componenti la brigata in una cronaca perugina del trecento.* Siena: Edizioni Cantagalli, 1991.

Navone, Giulio, ed. *Le rime di Folgore da San Gemignano e di Cene da la Chitarra d'Arezzo.* Bologna: Romagnoli, 1880.

Neri, Ferdinando, ed. *I sonetti di Folgore da San Gimignano.* Città del Castello: Lapi, 1914.

Orvieto, Paolo, and Brestolini, Lucia. *La poesia comico-realistica: dalle origini al Cinquecento.* Roma: Carocci, 2000.

Pepin, Ronald E. *Scorn for the World: Bernard of Cluny's* De contemptu mundi. *The Latin Text with English Translation and an Introduction*. East Lansing MI: Medieval Texts and Studies, 1991.

Perrus, Claude. "Courtoisie et décadence dans la poésie de Folgore da San Gimignano." *Revue des études italiennes* 9 (1962): 5–32.

Petrocchi, Giorgio. "I poeti realisti." In *Storia della letteratura italiana*, vol. 1, *Le origini e il Duecento*. Edited by Emilio Cecchi and Natalino Sapegno. Milano: Garzanti, 1965. 689–725.

Picone, Michelangelo. "La brigata di Folgore fra Dante e Boccaccio." In *Il giuoco della vita bella: Folgore da San Gimignano: studi e testi*. Edited by Michelangelo Picone. San Gimignano: Città di San Gimignano, 1988. 25–40.

———. "Il giuoco della vita bella." In *Il giuoco della vita bella: Folgore da San Gimignano: studi e testi*. Edited by Michelangelo Picone. San Gimignano: Città di San Gimignano, 1988. 7–11.

Pont, Maria. "Sonetti per l'armamento di un cavaliere." In *Il giuoco della vita bella: Folgore da San Gimignano: studi e testi*. Edited by Michelangelo Picone. San Gimignano: Città di San Gimignano, 1988. 51–63.

Ragni, Eugenio. "Brigata Spendereccia." In *Enciclopedia Dantesca*, vol. 1. Roma: Istituto della Enciclopedia Italiana, 1970. 699–700.

Rossetti, Dante Gabriel. *The Early Italian Poets From Ciullo D'Alcamo to Dante Alighieri (1100–1200–1300)*. London: Smith, Elder, and Co., 1861. 330–45.

Sanesi, Ireneo. "Fòlgore o Folgòre?" *Lingua Nostra* 22 (1961): 66–71.

Santucci, Luigi. *Folgore da San Gimignano*. Firenze: Sansoni, 1942.

Sapegno, Natalino. "Poesia realistica e borghese." In *Il Trecento*. Milano: Vallardi, 1973. 63–108.

Suitner, Franco. *La poesia satirica e giocosa nell'età dei comuni*. Padova: Antenore, 1983.

Toynbee, Paget. "Brigata Spendereccia." In *Concise Dictionary of Proper Names and Notable Matters in the Works of Dante*. New York: Phaeton Press, 1968. 92.

Trexler, Richard C. "Correre la Terra: Collective Insults in the Late Middle Ages." In *Dependence in Context in Renaissance Florence*. Binghamton, NY: Medieval & Renaissance Texts and Studies, 1994. 113–70.

Tusiani, Joseph. *The Age of Dante: An Anthology of Early Italian Poetry*. New York: Baroque Press, 1974. 40–49.

Valentini, Rosella Omicciolo. *Mangiare nelle taverne medievali tra cibo, vino e giochi*. Tuscania: Edizioni penne e papiri, 2007.

Vitale, Maurizio. *La lingua dei poeti realistico-giocosi del '200 e del '300*. Milano: La Goliardica, 1955.

———, ed. *Rimatori comico-realistici del Due e Trecento*. Torino: UTET, 1956.

Walsh, P. G. "Antifeminism in the High Middle Ages." In *Satiric Advice on Women and Marriage: From Plautus to Chaucer*. Edited by Warren S. Smith. Ann Arbor, MI: The University of Michigan Press, 2005. 222–42.

Weinstein, Donald. "Writing the Book on Italian Anticlericalism." In *Anticlericalism in Late Medieval and Early Modern Europe*. Edited by Peter A. Dykema and Heiko A. Oberman. Leiden, New York, Köln: E. J. Brill, 1993. 309–13.

Wilson, Katharina M., and Elizabeth M. Makowski. *Wykked Wyves and the Woes of Marriage: Misogamous Literature from Juvenal to Chaucer.* Albany, NY: State University of New York Press, 1990.

Zilli, Anna Paola. "Le rime di Pietro de' Faitinelli." *Quaderni lucchesi* 1:1 (gennaio-giugno 2000): 11–104.

Chapter One: Folgore da San Gimignano (ca. 1265–75 / ca. 1332)

Sonnets of the Months (Sonnets #1–14): A *corona* of sonnets that represents the activities of a group of fictional medieval nobles. It is addressed to Niccolò di Nisi, frequently identified as Niccolò di Dionigi of San Gimignano (ca. 1309), a member of the Salimbeni family. Folgore lists other members of Niccolò's group about whom almost nothing is known: Tengoccio, who may be Tengoccio di Baldo Grosso de' Tolomei (ca. 1323); Mugàvero, possibly Mogavero del Balza (ca. 1326); and Fainotto, who may be Fainotto di Guido Squarcialupi (ca. 1320). The other individuals—Ancaiano, Bartolo, and Min di Tengo—are unidentified.

1. Sonnets of the Months: Introduction

To the noble and courteous company
in whichever places they happen to be
living in joy, I always donate
dogs, birds, and money for expenses,
laden workhorses, quails hunted in flight,
hounds unleashed, greyhounds running with abandon.
I crown Niccolò[1] in this kingdom
because he's the flower of Siena,
Tengoccio, and Min di Tengo, and Ancaiano,
Bartolo with Mugàvero and Fainotto,
who all seem to be King Priam's children,
bolder and more courtly than Lancelot.

[1] In the last sonnet of the months, this individual is specified as Niccolò di Nisi. Recently, Ubaldo Morandi proposed another individual, Niccolò di Nici of the Tolomei (ca. 1290–1340), a family enimical to the Salimbeni.

1. Sonetti de' mesi[1]: Introduzione

A la brigata nobele[2] e cortese
en[3] tutte quelle parte,[4] dove sono
con allegrezza[5] stando, sempre dono
cani, uccelli e danari[6] per ispese,
ronzin portanti, quaglie[7] a volo prese
bracchi levar, correr veltri a bandono:[8]
in questo regno Niccolò[9] corono,
per ch'ell'è 'l fior[10] de la[11] città sanese;
Tengoccio e Min di Tengo ed[12] Ancaiano,
Bartolo con[13] Mugàvero[14] e Fainotto,
che paiono figliuoi[15] del re Priàno,
prodi e cortesi[16] più che Lancilotto;

---

[1] For *lectiones* of the sonnets of the months based upon a fourteenth-century Perugian manuscript, alongside facsimiles of the codex, see *I sonetti dei mesi ed i componenti la brigata in una cronaca perugina del Trecento*, ed., Ubaldo Morandi (Siena: Edizioni Cantagalli, 1991).

[2] Navone, Neri, Massèra, Vitale, and Caravaggi: "nobile."

[3] Massèra and Vitale: "e 'n."

[4] Massèra, Vitale, and Caravaggi: "parti."

[5] Neri: "alegrezza."

[6] Vitale: "danar."

[7] Navone: "quagle."

[8] Navone: "a-bbandono." Neri: "abbandono."

[9] Navone, Neri, and Caravaggi: "Nicolò."

[10] Navone and Neri: "egli è 'l fior." Massèra: "elli è fior." Caravaggi: "elli è 'l fior."

[11] Caravaggi: "della."

[12] Navone: "et."

[13] Navone and Caravaggi: "e."

[14] Neri: "Bartolo Mugavero."

[15] Navone: "figloli." Neri: "figlioi." Caravaggi: "figliuol."

[16] Neri: "prodi, cortesi."

If necessary, with lances in their hands,
they would hold tournaments in Camelot.

2. Sonnets of the Months: January

I give you, in the month of January,
courts with fires and lighted halls,
chambers and beds with all the nice luxuries,
sheets of silk and coverlets of ermine,
jellies and desserts and strong wines,
clothes from Douaix and wool from Rascia;
in this way, they'd be prepared even if
the South Wind, West Wind, or North Wind blew.
To go out several times during the day
throwing the white and pretty snow
at the damsels who are all about.
And when the company felt tired,
they would return to this court —
so may the honest company find rest.

se bisognasse, con le lance in mano
farìano[1] torneamenti[2] a Camelotto.

2. Sonetti de' mesi: Di gennaio

I' doto voi, nel[3] mese di[4] gennaio,
corte con fòchi[5] di salette accese,
camer'e[6] letta d'ogni bello arnese,
lenzuol' de[7] seta e copertoi di vaio,
tregèa, confetti e mescere arazzaio,[8]
vestiti di doagio[9] e di rascese:[10]
e 'n questo modo star[11] a le defese,
mova[12] scirocco,[13] garbino o rovaio.
Uscir di fòr[14] alcuna volta il giorno,
gittando de la[15] neve bella e bianca
a le[16] donzelle che staran da torno;
e quando fosse la compagna stanca,
a questa corte faciase retorno:[17]
e si[18] riposi la brigata franca.

---

[1] Massèra, Vitale, and Caravaggi: "farìan."
[2] Neri: "torniamenti."
[3] Caravaggi: "del."
[4] Neri: "de."
[5] Massèra and Caravaggi: "fuochi."
[6] Navone: "camere." Neri and Caravaggi: "camere e."
[7] Navone and Neri: "lenzuol de." Massèra and Vitale: "lenzuoi di." Caravaggi: "lenzuol di."
[8] Navone: "arazaio." Massèra, Vitale, and Caravaggi: "a razzaio."
[9] Navone: "doasio."
[10] Caravaggi: "racese."
[11] Neri, Vitale, and Caravaggi: "stare."
[12] Massèra and Caravaggi: "muova."
[13] Neri: "sirocco."
[14] Navone and Neri: "for'," Massèra and Caravaggi: "fuor."
[15] Navone and Caravaggi: "della."
[16] Caravaggi: "alle."
[17] Navone and Neri: "facciase ritorno." Massèra, Vitale, and Caravaggi: "facciasi ritorno."
[18] Caravaggi: "sì."

3. Sonnets of the Months: February

And in February I give you good hunts
of deer, of roe bucks, and of wild boars,
short hunting skirts, and thick woolen leggings,
and companions who amuse and please you;
hounds off leashes, and tracking dogs in pursuit;
and purses well furnished with money,
in spite of the cheap and the greedy,
or whoever gets in your way about it.
To come home in the evening with your attendants
loaded down with so much wild game,
with joy and gaiety and singing;
to have draughts of wine and a steaming kitchen,
and remain radiant until sleep comes,
and then to rest until the morning.

4. Sonnets of the Months: March

For March I give you a fishing pier
with eels, trouts, lampreys, and salmon,
with snappers, dolphins, and sturgeons,
and every other fish along the shore;
with fishermen and boats all in array,
and ships, cutters, and galleons,

3. Sonetti de' mesi: Di febbraio

E de febbrai'[1] vi dono bella caccia
di cervi, di cavrioli[2] e di cinghiari,
corte gonnelle, e[3] grossi calzari,
e compagnia che ve deletti[4] e piaccia;
can da guinzagli e segugi da traccia,
e le borse fornite di danari,
ad onta degli scarsi e degli avari,
o di chi 'n[5] questo vi dà[6] briga e 'mpaccia.
E la sera tornar co' vostri fanti
carcati de la molta selvaggina,[7]
avendo gioia ed allegrezza[8] e canti;
far trar del vino e fumar la cucina,
e fin al primo sonno star razzanti:[9]
e po' posare 'nfin[10] a la[11] mattina.[12]

4. Sonetti de' mesi: Di marzo

Di marzo sì vi do una pischiera[13]
d'anguille, trote,[14] lamprede e salmoni,
di dèntici,[15] dalfini, e storïoni,
d'ogn'altro pesce in tutta la rivèra;[16]
con pescatori e navicelle a schiera
e barche, saettìe e galeoni,

---

[1] Navone: "De febraio." Neri: "E di febraio." Vitale and Caravaggi: "E di febbraio."

[2] Caravaggi: "di cerbi, di cavrïuoli."

[3] Navone, Neri, Massèra, Vitale, and Caravaggi: "gonnelle con."

[4] Navone and Neri: "ve deletta." Massèra and Caravaggi: "vi diletti." Vitale: "vi diletta."

[5] Navone, Neri, and Caravaggi: "o chi di."

[6] Navone: "da." Massèra: "dán."

[7] Navone and Neri: "salvagina." Massèra, Vitale, and Caravaggi: "salvaggina."

[8] Neri: "gioia, alegrezza."

[9] Navone and Neri: "raggianti."

[10] Navone and Neri: "po' posar enfin." Caravaggi: "poi posar infin'."

[11] Caravaggi: "alla."

[12] Navone: "matina."

[13] Massèra, Vitale, and Caravaggi: "peschiera."

[14] Caravaggi: "di trote, anguille."

[15] Massèra and Neri: "dèntali." Navone and Vitale: "dentali."

[16] Caravaggi: "riviera."

which can carry you in any season
to any port you desire right away;
  and may it be filled with many palaces
and every other thing that you might need,
and may all your people have only pleasure.
  May there not be a church or monastery —
let the crazy priests preach their sermons,
for they tell many lies and speak little truth.[1]

5. Sonnets of the Months: April

  In April I give you the gentle countryside
flowering with beautiful fresh herbs,
fountains of water, which don't weary you,
ladies and damsels as your companions,
  ambling palfreys, Spanish chargers,
and people clothed in the French manner,
to sing and to dance in the Provençal way,
with new instruments from Germany.
  And may there be many gardens all around,
and may everyone be humble towards you:

[1] Anticlericalism is a commonplace of medieval comic poetry, but Donald Weinstein argues that it would be a mistake to view it as a timeless feature; rather, anticlericalism often appears in literature as a response to specific events. The anticlerical ending of the March sonnet may reflect historical developments during the years of the *corona*'s composition. Nicolino Applauso notes that the war between San Gimignano and Volterra in 1308 resulted in increased tensions with the Church. The clergy of San Gimignano refused to pay the taxes levied to fund the war, causing a public scandal. See Donald Weinstein, "Writing the Book on Italian Anticlericalism." In *Anticlericalism in Late Medieval and Early Modern Europe* (Leiden, New York, Köln: E. J. Brill, 1993): 309–13 (310); and Nicolino Applauso, "Folgore da San Gimignano e la parodia di Cenne: intrighi politici e poetici," in *La poesia italiana prima di Dante*, 251–53.

le qual ve portino a tutte stagioni[1]
a qual porto vi piace a la primèra:[2]
    che sia fornito de molti palazzi,
d'ogn'altra cosa che ve[3] sie mestèro,[4]
e gente v'abbia[5] de[6] tutti[7] solazzi.
    Chiesia[8] non[9] v'abbia[10] mai nè monastero;
lassate[11] predicar i preti pazzi,[12]
c'hanno troppe[13] bugie e poco vero.

5. Sonetti de' mesi: Di aprile

    D'aprile[14] vi dono la gentil campagna
tutta fiorita di bell'erba fresca:
fontane d'acqua che non vi rincresca,
donn'e[15] donzelle per vostra compagna,
    ambianti palafren, destrier di Spagna[16]
e gente costumata a la[17] francesca;
cantar, danzar a la[18] provenzalesca
con istrumenti novi[19] d'Alemagna.
    E da torno vi sia[20] molti giardini
e giacchito[21] vi sia ogni persona:

[1] Navone: "le qual ve porteno tutte stasoni." Neri: "le qual se portino tutte stagioni." Massèra and Vitale: "le quai vi portino tutte stagioni." Caravaggi: "le qual vi portino a tutte stagioni."
[2] Caravaggi: "primiera."
[3] Massèra, Vitale, and Caravaggi: "vi."
[4] Navone, Neri, and Caravaggi: "mestiero."
[5] Navone: "v'abia."
[6] Massèra, Vitale, and Caravaggi: "di."
[7] Massèra: "tutt'i'."
[8] Massèra, Vitale, and Caravaggi: "Chiesa."
[9] Neri: "no."
[10] Navone: "v'abia."
[11] Caravaggi: "lasciate."
[12] Navone: "pazi."
[13] Caravaggi: "ché hanno assai."
[14] Navone, Neri, Massèra, Vitale, and Caravaggi: "D'april."
[15] Navone, Neri, and Caravaggi: "donne e."
[16] Navone: "Spagnia."
[17] Caravaggi: "alla."
[18] Caravaggi: "alla."
[19] Navone and Neri: "istormenti novi." Caravaggi: "istormenti nuovi."
[20] Navone: "dintorno vi sian." Caravaggi: "d'attorno vi sian."
[21] Navone and Neri: "giachita."

may everyone love, and bow with reverence to,
the noble man, whom I gave the crown
with precious stones—the very finest
that Prester John or Babylon's king have.

6. Sonnets of the Months: May

In May I give you many horses,
all of them are obedient to the reins,
gallopers all, straight runners,
wearing chest armor, bridles with bells,
banners with coverings of many designs,
and silks of all different colors;
shields in the manner of warriors,
violets, roses, flowers that dazzle everyone;
and to break and ruin spears and lances,
and down from the windows and balconies
rain garlands, and oranges are tossed back up;
and young maidens and pageboys
kiss each other on the lips and cheeks
and speak of love and pleasures.

7. Sonnets of the Months: June

In June I give you a small mountain
covered with beautiful little trees,

ciascun con reverenza adori e 'nchini
a quel gentil, c'ho dato la corona
de[1] pietre prezïose, le più fini
c'ha[2] 'l presto Gianni o 'l re de Babilòna.

6. Sonetti de' mesi: Di Maggio

Di maggio sì vi do molti cavagli
e tutti quanti siano[3] affrenatori,
portanti tutti, dritti corritori;
pettorali, testère[4] de[5] sonagli,
bandère con[6] coverte a molti 'ntagli[7]
di zendadi e di[8] tutti li colori;
le targhe a modo degli armeggiatori;
viuole,[9] rose,[10] fior, ch'ogn'om[11] abbagli;
e rompere[12] e fiaccar bigordi e lance,
e piover da fenestre e da balconi
en[13] giù ghirlande, e 'n[14] sù melarance;
e pulzellette gioveni[15] e garzoni
baciarsi ne la bocca e ne le guance:
d'amor e di goder vi si ragioni.[16]

7. Sonetti de' mesi: Di giugno

Di giugno dovvi[17] una montagnetta
coverta di belli[18] arboscelli,

---

[1] Caravaggi: "di."
[2] Neri: "ch'à."
[3] Caravaggi: "sieno."
[4] Caravaggi: "testiere."
[5] Navone and Neri: "con." Massèra, Vitale, and Caravaggi: "di."
[6] Neri and Caravaggi: "bandiere e."
[7] Navone and Caravaggi: "intagli." Massèra and Vitale: "tagli."
[8] Caravaggi: "e di zendadi di."
[9] Massèra: "viol'e." Neri, Navone, and Vitale: "viole." Caravaggi: "viole e."
[10] Massèra: "ros'e." Caravaggi: "rose e."
[11] Navone, Massèra, Vitale, and Caravaggi: "uom."
[12] Neri: "Rompere."
[13] Massèra, Vitale, and Caravaggi: "in."
[14] Navone: "e in." Massèra, Vitale, and Caravaggi: "ed in."
[15] Navone and Neri: "giovene." Caravaggi: "e giovani."
[16] Navone: "rasoni."
[17] Navone and Neri: "dovi."
[18] Neri: "coverta di bellissimi." Caravaggi: "coperta di bellissimi."

with thirty villas and twelve castles
which surround a small village;
    it has at its center a small spring
that makes a thousand creeks and rivulets,
cutting through the gardens and meadows
to bring refreshment to the short grass.
    May orange trees and cedars, date trees and lemons
and all the other flavorful fruits
be hung on pergolas along the roads;
    and may everyone there be in love
and treat each other with so much courtesy
that the whole world will see them as gracious.

8. Sonnets of the Months: July

    For July, in Siena, on the paved streets,
with goblets full of trebbiano wine
in the cellars, and ice-cold vaiano wine,
with the company, mornings and evenings;
    to eat some of that abundant jelly,
roasted partridges, young pheasants,

con trenta ville e dodici castelli,
che sian[1] entorno[2] ad una cittadetta,
ch'abbia nel mezzo una soa[3] fontanetta:
e faccia mille rami e fiumicelli,
ferendo per giardin[4] e praticelli
e rinfrescando[5] la menuta[6] erbetta.
Aranci e cedri,[7] dàttili e lumie
e tutte l'altre frutte savorose
empergolate[8] siano[9] per le vie;
e le genti[10] vi sian[11] tutte amorose
e faccianvisi tante cortesie,
ch'a tutto 'l mondo siano[12] grazïose.

8. Sonetti de' mesi: Di luglio

Di luglio en[13] Siena su[14] la saliciata,
con le piene enghestare de tribbiani,[15]
ne le[16] cantine li ghiacci vaiani;
e man[17] e sera mangiar[18] in brigata
di quella gelatina ismisurata,
istarne roste,[19] giovene[20] fagiani,

---

[1] Navone and Neri: "siano." Caravaggi: "sieno."
[2] Massèra, Vitale, and Caravaggi: "intorno."
[3] Navone, Massèra, Vitale, and Caravaggi: "sua." Neri: "so'."
[4] Navone and Neri: "firendo per giardini." Caravaggi: "ferendo per giardini."
[5] Navone: "rifrescando."
[6] Navone, Neri, Massèra, Vitale, and Caravaggi: "minuta."
[7] Navone and Neri: "aranci, cedri."
[8] Massèra, Vitale, and Caravaggi: "impergolate."
[9] Caravaggi: "sieno."
[10] Navone: "gente."
[11] Caravaggi: "sien."
[12] Caravaggi: "sieno."
[13] Massèra, Vitale, and Caravaggi: "in."
[14] Navone: "in su." Caravaggi: "in sulla."
[15] Massèra and Vitale: "con piene le 'nghistare di trebbiani." Navone and Neri: "con le piene enghestare de tribiani." Caravaggi: "con le piene inguistare de' trebbiani."
[16] Caravaggi: "nelle."
[17] Navone and Neri: "man'."
[18] Caravaggi: "mangiare."
[19] Caravaggi: "arrosto."
[20] Massèra and Vitale: "gioveni." Caravaggi: "e giovani."

boiled capons, and superior goat-kids,
and, for whoever likes it, veal with garlic sauce.
And to pass good times, and a good life there,
and not to go out because of the heat,
to wear fine silks of high quality,
and when you rejoice, to remain firm and solid,
and always to have a well-furnished table,
and not to want a wife as a chaperone.

9. Sonnets of the Months: August

In August I give you thirty castles
in a mountainous alpine valley
hidden from the ocean winds
so you can be healthy, shining like stars;
and to mount the saddles of palfreys,
and to ride in the evenings and mornings,
and cities nearby to one another
so that your day's ride is only a mile.
Returning all the while toward home;
and may a river run through the valley
that goes night and day strong and clean;
and to stay outdoors during midday.
Your purses should always be open-mouthed
for the best food of all of Tuscany.

lessi capponi, capretti[1] sovrani
e cui piacesse, manza[2] con[3] l'agliata.
Ed ine trar bon tempo e bona vita,[4]
e non andar de fòr[5] per questo caldo;
vestir zendadi di bella partita;
e quando godi, star pur fermo e saldo,
e sempre aver la tavola fornita:
e non voler la moglie per gastaldo.

9. Sonetti de' mesi: D'agosto

D'agosto sì vi do trenta castella
in una valle d'alpe montanina,
che non vi possa vento de[6] marina,
per istar sani, chiari[7] come stella;
e palafreni da[8] montare 'n[9] sella
e cavalcar la sera e la mattina:
e l'una terra a l'altra[10] sia vicina,
ch'un miglio sia la vostra giornatella,
tornando tuttavia inverso[11] casa;
e per la valle corre[12] una fiumana,
che vada notte e dì traente e rasa;
e star nel fresco tutta meriggiana.
La vostra borsa sempre a bocca pasa,
per la miglior vivanda di Toscana.

---

1 Caravaggi: "e capretti."

2 Navone, Neri, and Caravaggi: "la manza."

3 Navone, Neri, Massèra, Vitale, and Caravaggi: "e."

4 Navone: "E vie trarre bon tempo e bona vita." Neri: "Et ive trar bon tempo e bona vita." Massèra, Vitale, and Caravaggi: "Ed ivi trar buon tempo e buona vita."

5 Massèra and Vitale: "andar di fuor." Caravaggi: "uscir di fuor."

6 Massèra, Vitale, and Caravaggi: "di."

7 Navone, Neri, and Caravaggi: "e chiari."

8 Navone: "de."

9 Caravaggi: "in."

10 Caravaggi: "all'altra."

11 Navone and Neri: "tutta via verso." Massèra and Vitale: "tuttavia verso la." Caravaggi: "tuttavïa verso."

12 Navone, Neri, Massèra, Vitale, and Caravaggi: "corra."

10. Sonnets of the Months: September

In September I give you many delights:
falcons, astors, pigeon hawks, and larks,
leather strips, jesses on their legs, rings with lures,
hunting dogs with bells, treats and gloves,
arrows, crossbows straight and accurate,
bows, darts, bolts, and archers,
may you have moulting sparrowhawks and astors
in the nest, and all others in flight
that catch birds in the nest and on the wing;
and everyone still giving to one another,
and may they play and not quarrel;
when you encounter other people,
may your purse always be ready for spending,
and may greediness always be cast out.

10. Sonetti de' mesi: Di settembre

Di settembre vi do deletti[1] tanti:
falconi, astori, smerletti, sparvieri;
lunghe, gherbegli, geti[2] con carnieri,
bracchetti con sonagli, pasto[3] e guanti;
bolze,[4] balestre dritt'e[5] ben portanti,
archi, strali, ballotte e ballottieri,
sìanvi mudati guilfanghi[6] ed[7] astieri
nidaci[8] e di tutt'altri uccel volanti,
che fosser boni[9] da snidar[10] e prendere:
e l'un l'altro[11] tuttavia[12] donando,[13]
e possasi rubar[14] e non contendere;
quando con altra gente rencontrando,[15]
la vostra borsa si'[16] acconcia[17] a spendere
e 'n tutto[18] abbiate l'avarizia en[19] bando.

---

[1] Massèra, Vitale, and Caravaggi: "diletti."
[2] Caravaggi: "e geti."
[3] Caravaggi: "pasti."
[4] Neri, Massèra, and Vitale: "bolz'e."
[5] Navone and Neri: "dritte." Caravaggi: "dritte e."
[6] Caravaggi: "girfalchi."
[7] Neri: "e."
[8] Navone: "nidace."
[9] Massèra, Vitale, and Caravaggi: "buoni."
[10] Navone and Neri: "d'assediare."
[11] Caravaggi: "all'altro."
[12] Navone: "tutta via."
[13] Massèra: "domando."
[14] Caravaggi: "rubare."
[15] Massèra, Vitale, and Caravaggi: "rincontrando."
[16] Navone and Neri: "sia."
[17] Caravaggi: "le vostre borse sempre acconce."
[18] Neri and Caravaggi: "e tutti."
[19] Massèra, Vitale, and Caravaggi: "in."

11. Sonnets of the Months: October

In October, in the county where there's good lodging,
I beg you, sons, to go there:
and have good weather and go hawking
as you like, on foot and on horseback.
In the evening go to the hall to dance
and drink some wine must and get drunk
because there is no better life, in truth:
this is as true as the florin is golden!
And then arise in the morning
and wash your faces with your hands;
roasts and wine are good medicine.
By the Gospels, you will be healthier
than a fish in a lake or river or ocean
having the best lives of any Christians.

11. Sonetti de' mesi: D'ottobre

Di ottobre[1] nel contà c'ha[2] buono stallo,
e' pregovi, figliuoi,[3] che voi n'andate;[4]
traetevi bon[5] tempo ed uccellate
come vi piace, a piè ed[6] a cavallo.
La sera per la sala andate[7] a ballo,
e bevete del mosto ed[8] inebriate,[9]
ché non ci ha[10] miglior vita, en[11] veritate:
e questo è vero[12] come 'l fiorin[13] giallo.
E poscia vi levate[14] la mattina,[15]
e lavativ'el[16] viso con le mani;
lo rosto[17] e 'l vino è bona[18] medicina.
A le[19] guagnèle, starete più sani,
ca[20] pesce in lag'o[21] fiume o[22] in marina,
avendo meglior[23] vita di[24] cristiani!

---

1 Navone and Caravaggi: "D'ottobre." Neri: "De ottobre."
2 Navone: "conta' c'ha." Neri: "contà c'à." Vitale: "contado a." Caravaggi: "contado ha."
3 Navone: "fregovi, figloli." Caravaggi: "pregovi, figliuol."
4 Caravaggi: "v'andiate."
5 Massèra, Vitale, and Caravaggi: "buon."
6 Navone and Neri: "piè et." Caravaggi: "piede ed."
7 Neri: "andati."
8 Navone, Massèra, Vitale, and Caravaggi: "e." Neri: "et."
9 Navone: "v'enibriate."
10 Neri: "à."
11 Massèra, Vitale, and Caravaggi: "in."
12 Neri and Caravaggi: "ver."
13 Navone and Caravaggi: "fiorino è." Neri: "fiorino."
14 Neri: "levati."
15 Navone and Neri: "matina."
16 Navone, Massèra, Vitale, and Caravaggi: "lavatevi 'l." Neri: "lavative 'l."
17 Caravaggi: "l'arrosto."
18 Massèra, Vitale, and Caravaggi: "buona."
19 Caravaggi: "Alle."
20 Neri and Caravaggi: "che."
21 Navone and Caravaggi: "lago o 'n." Neri: "lago o."
22 Caravaggi: "od."
23 Navone: "meglor." Caravaggi: "miglior."
24 Caravaggi: "che."

12. Sonnets of the Months: November

And in November at the baths of Petriuolo
with thirty mules laden with money,
may the silkworm be wrapped up in silk;
silver cups, and flasks of tin;
To give all the merchants their earnings:
torches, candles that come from Chiareta,
and candied sorbets from Gaeta —
may everyone drink and comfort their companions.
And though the cold be fierce the fires are hot:
pheasants, partridges, doves, and mincemeats,
hares and roe bucks, roasted and boiled;
and to always have good appetites,
and at night the winds and rain come from the sky
but may you be well furnished in your beds.

12. Sonetti de' mesi: Di novembre

E di novembre a Petrïuolo al[1] bagno,
con trenta muli carchi de[2] moneta:
la ruga sia tutta coverta[3] a seta;
coppe d'argento, bottacci di stagno:
e dar[4] a tutti[5] stazzonier[6] guadagno;
torchi, doppier che vegnan[7] di Chiareta;
confetti con cedrata de[8] Gaeta;
e béa ciascun[9] e conforti 'l compagno.
E 'l freddo vi sia[10] grande e 'l fòco[11] spesso;
fagiani,[12] starne, colombi, mortiti,[13]
lèvori, cavrïoli rosto[14] e lesso:
e sempre aver[15] acconci gli[16] appetiti;
la notte 'l vento, 'l[17] piover a ciel[18] messo:
e siate[19] ne le[20] letta ben forniti.

---

[1] Massèra and Vitale: "il."
[2] Massèra, Vitale, and Caravaggi: "di."
[3] Caravaggi: "le rughe sien tutte coperte."
[4] Caravaggi: "dare."
[5] Navone: "tutti i."
[6] Neri: "i stazonier."
[7] Caravaggi: "torchi e doppier che vengan." Neri: "torchi, doppier che vegna."
[8] Neri and Caravaggi: "di."
[9] Caravaggi: "bëa ciascuno."
[10] Massèra and Vitale: "E lo freddo sia grande." Neri: "E 'l freddo sia grande."
[11] Massèra, Vitale, and Caravaggi: "fuoco."
[12] Navone: "fasani."
[13] Caravaggi: "e mortiti."
[14] Caravaggi: "e cavriuoli arrosto."
[15] Caravaggi: "avere."
[16] Navone: "gl'."
[17] Massèra and Vitale: "e." Caravaggi: "e 'l."
[18] Navone and Neri: "cel."
[19] Neri: "siati."
[20] Caravaggi: "nelle."

13. Sonnets of the Months: December

And in December, a city on the plain,
halls on the ground floor, giant fires,
rugs spread out, game tables and gambling,
burning candles—to stay up with dice in hand.
And a drunk, gluttonous barkeeper,
slaughtered pigs and the finest cooks,
tasty morsels, may everyone drink and eat.
May the casks be broader than the town of San Galgano.
And may you be well-dressed and bundled
with robes, cloaks, and mantles
wearing fine priceless hoods;
and to make fun of the all the sad and miserable,
all the pained, unhappy and unfortunate
avaricious: may you have nothing to do with them.

13. Sonetti de' mesi: Di decembre

E di decembre[1] una città in[2] piano:
sale terrene, grandissimi fòchi,[3]
tappeti[4] tesi, tavolier[5] e giochi,[6]
torticci accesi, star[7] co' dadi[8] en[9] mano,
e l'oste inebrïato[10] e catellano,
e porci morti e finissimi[11] còchi,[12]
ghiotti morselli, ciascun béa e mandóchi:[13]
le botte sian[14] maggior che[15] San Galgano.
E siate ben vestiti e foderati
di guarnacche, tabarri e di mantegli[16]
e di cappucci fini e smesurati;[17]
e beffe far de'[18] tristi cattivegli,[19]
de' miseri dolenti sciagurati
avari: non vogliate usar con egli.[20]

---

[1] Massèra, Vitale, and Caravaggi: "dicembre."
[2] Navone and Neri: "en."
[3] Massèra and Caravaggi: "fuochi."
[4] Navone: "tappedi."
[5] Caravaggi: "tavolieri."
[6] Massèra and Caravaggi: "giuochi."
[7] Caravaggi: "e star."
[8] Navone: "dati."
[9] Massèra, Vitale, and Caravaggi: "in."
[10] Navone: "enbriaco." Neri: "embriaco."
[11] Navone and Neri: "fenissimi."
[12] Massèra and Caravaggi: "cuochi."
[13] Caravaggi: "e morselli ciascun, bèa e manuchi."
[14] Neri: "la botte sia." Caravaggi: "le botti sien."
[15] Massèra and Vitale: "botti sien maggior ch'a."
[16] Massèra and Vitale: "di guarnacch'e tabarri e di mantelli." Navone, Neri, and Caravaggi: "di guarnacche, tabarri e di mantelli."
[17] Navone, Neri, Massèra, Vitale, and Caravaggi: "smisurati."
[18] Navone and Neri: "dei."
[19] Navone, Neri, Massèra, Vitale, and Caravaggi: "cattivelli."
[20] Navone, Neri, Massèra, Vitale, and Caravaggi: "elli."

14. Sonnets of the Months: Conclusion

My sonnet, say to Niccolò di Nisi,
the man who's full of all nobility,
on my behalf, with great joyfulness,
that I am fulfilled with all his services.
And it is worth more to me than all Paris
to have his friendship and his loyalty;
if he had all the riches of the Empire
he'd be worthier than Saint Francis of Assisi.
Commend me to him at all hours,
and to his companion, and Ancaiano,
because without him no company is joyful.
Your Folgore of San Gimignano
sends you, commands, and makes the entreaty
that you go with his heart in your hand.

14. Sonetti de' mesi: Conclusione

Sonetto mio, a Niccolò[1] di Nisi,
colui ch'è pien de[2] tutta gentilezza,[3]
dì da mia parte con molt'allegrezza[4]
che eo so' acconcio a tutti soi[5] servisi;
e più m'è caro che non val Parisi,
d'avere[6] sua amistade e contezza:[7]
se ello avesse emperïal[8] ricchezza,[9]
stare' li[10] me'[11] che San Francesco[12] en[13] Sisi.
Raccomendame[14] a lui tutta fïata
ed[15] a la so'[16] compagna ed[17] Ancaiano,
ché senza lui non è lieta brigata.
Folgore vostro da San Giminiano[18]
vi manda, dice e fa questa[19] ambasciata:
che voi n'andaste[20] con su' cor en[21] mano.

---

[1] Navone: "Nicholò." Neri and Caravaggi: "Nicolò."

[2] Caravaggi: "di."

[3] Navone: "gentileza."

[4] Navone: "molta allegreza." Neri: "molt'alegrezza."

[5] Navone: "ch'eo sono acconcio a tutt'i suoi." Neri: "ch'eo sono acconcio a tutt'i so'." Massèra: "ch'io son acconcio a tutt'i suoi." Vitale and Caravaggi: "ch'io son acconcio a tutti suoi."

[6] Navone and Neri: "d'aver."

[7] Navone: "conteza."

[8] Massèra and Vitale: "e s'ello avesse imperïal." Neri: "e s'ello avesse emperial." Caravaggi: "sed ello avesse imperïal."

[9] Navone: "riccheza."

[10] Caravaggi: "starieli."

[11] Navone: "meglo." Neri: "meglio."

[12] Neri: "che Francesco."

[13] Caravaggi: "in."

[14] Navone and Neri: "Racomendame." Massèra, Vitale, and Caravaggi: "Raccomendami."

[15] Neri: "et."

[16] Navone, Massèra, Vitale, and Caravaggi: "sua."

[17] Neri: "et."

[18] Navone: "Geminiano."

[19] Caravaggi: "quest'."

[20] Neri: "n'andasti."

[21] Navone: "suo core en." Neri: "so' cor en." Massèra, Vitale, and Caravaggi: "suo cor in."

Sonnets of the Days (Sonnets #15–22): The second of Folgore's *corone*, which also deals with the activities of a fictional group of nobles. This sonnet cycle is dedicated to Carlo di Guerra Cavicciuoli (ca. 1308), a soldier in San Gimignano's war against Volterra. According to Folgore, Carlo is as generous as Azzo III of the Este (d. 1308), whom he refers to as "the Lombard Marquis."

15. Days of the Week: Introduction

I decided to make a necklace
which would be gay, joyful, and ornate,
and I'd so like to donate it, in part or whole,
so everyone would say "it's worthy of him, it's beautiful."
And now I've found a young pageboy,
wise, courteous, and well instructed,
who'd be more worthy of an imperial treasure
than a jewel needs a setting on a ring.
Carlo di messer Guerra Cavicciuoli,
who is valiant, brave, and daring,
as servants he should command whomever he wants;
more sprightly than a wildcat or leopard
and he never held onto his coins as if children,
but he spends more than the Lombard marquis.

15. Sonetti de la semana: Introduzione

I' ho[1] pensato di far[2] un gioiello,
che si'[3] allegro,[4] gioioso ed[5] ornato,
e sì 'l vorrei donare 'n[6] parte e lato,
ch'ogn'uomo[7] dica: —E' li sta ben, è bello!—
E or di novo[8] ho[9] trovato un donzello
saggio, cortes'e ben[10] ammaestrato,[11]
che gli starebbe me'[12] l'emperïato,[13]
che non istà la gemma ne l'anello:[14]
Carlo di misser[15] Guerra Cavicciuoli,
quel ch'è valent'ed[16] ardito e gagliardo
e servente, comandi chi vuoli;[17]
leggero più che lonza o lïopardo:
e mai non[18] fece de' denar figliuoli,[19]
ma spende più che 'l marchese lombardo.

---

1 Navone: "I'o." Neri: "I'ò."
2 Caravaggi: "fare."
3 Navone, Neri, and Caravaggi: "sia."
4 Neri: "'legro."
5 Navone and Neri: "et."
6 Navone: "donar en." Caravaggi: "donare in."
7 Navone: "che ogni uom." Neri: "ch'ogn'uom."
8 Massèra, Vitale, and Caravaggi: "nuovo."
9 Navone and Neri: "ò."
10 Navone: "cortese, bene." Neri: "cortese, ben." Caravaggi: "cortese e ben."
11 Neri: "amaestrato."
12 Navone: "meglo." Massèra and Vitale: "meglio."
13 Caravaggi: "l'imperïato."
14 Navone and Caravaggi: "nell'anello."
15 Neri: "messer."
16 Navone and Neri: "valente."
17 Massèra, Neri, Vitale, and Caravaggi: "chi che vuoli."
18 Neri: "no."
19 Navone: "dei denar figluoli." Caravaggi: "dei denar figliuoli."

16. Sonnets of the Week: Monday

When the moon and the star of Venus
and the night disappear, and the day appears,
a light wind comes to clean the air
and make the people happy and healthy;
Monday, the beginning of the week,
with instruments to play a morning song
and to make the damsels sing in love,
and to have the sun radiate at noontime.
Arise, young pageboy and don't sleep
because the loving day comforts you,
and wants you to go and to serve your lady.
May a palfrey or charger be your mount,
pageboys and servants, with beautiful clothes;
and then do what Love commands.

17. Sonnets of the Months: Tuesday

And on Tuesday I give him a new world:
to hear trumpets and drums playing,
to arm footmen, knights, and pageboys,
and bells and clappers say "ding dong!"
He first, and the others following,
armed with cuirasses and with hats,
to see enemies and to strike them,

16. Sonetti de la semana: Lunidie

Quando la luna e la stella dïana
e la notte si parte e 'l giorno appare,
vento leggero, per polire l'are
e far[1] la gente star[2] allegra e sana;
il lunedì,[3] per capo di semana,
con instrumenti mattinata[4] fare,
ed[5] amorose donzelle cantare
e 'l sol ferire per la meridiana.
Lèvati sù, donzel,[6] e non dormire,
ché l'amoroso giorno ti conforta
e vòl[7] che vadi tua donn'a[8] servire.
Palafren[9] e distrier sian[10] a la porta,
donzelli e servitor con bel vestire:
e po' far[11] ciò ch'Amor comanda e porta.

17. Sonetti de la semana: Martidie

E 'l martedì[12] li do un nòvo[13] mondo:
udir sonar trombetti e tamburelli,
armar pedon, cavalier[14] e donzelli,
e campane a martello dicer "dòn do";
e lui primèro[15] e li[16] altri secondo,
armati de[17] loriche e di cappelli,
veder nemici e percoter[18] ad elli,

---

[1] Massèra: "ne fa."
[2] Caravaggi: "stare."
[3] Navone: "lunidì."
[4] Navone: "istormenti matinata." Neri: "instrumenti matinata." Caravaggi: "istormenti mattinata."
[5] Navone and Neri: "et."
[6] Navone, Neri, and Caravaggi: "donzello."
[7] Navone, Massèra, Vitale, and Caravaggi: "vuol."
[8] Caravaggi: "donna a."
[9] Navone and Caravaggi: "palafreni."
[10] Caravaggi: "sieno."
[11] Navone: "poi fa." Caravaggi: "poi far."
[12] Navone: "El martidì."
[13] Massèra, Vitale, and Caravaggi: "nuovo."
[14] Neri: "cavalieri."
[15] Neri, Massèra, Vitale, and Caravaggi: "primiero."
[16] Navone: "gli."
[17] Navone, Massèra, Vitale, and Caravaggi: "di."
[18] Caravaggi: "percuotere."

landing great blows and de-horsing them;
    to see steeds running with empty saddles
pulling their lords across the fields
and dragging behind livers and innards;
    and companies of buglers play
and whistles, flutes, and pipes,
and infantrymen return to their ranks.

18. Sonnets of the Week: Wednesday

    Every Wednesday, a great banquet
of hares, partridges, pheasants, and peacocks,
cooked beef and roasted capons,
and other foods that are as delicate;
    ladies and damsels are all around,
daughters of kings, of counts, of barons,
and maidens and young pageboys
serve while wearing amorous garlands;
    cups, chalices, gold and silver bowls,
Greek wine from the coast, and vernaccia,
fruits, and as many candies as you might want;
    to present you with hunted birds and wild game;

dando gran colpi e mettendoli a fondo;
    destrier veder andar[1] a voite[2] selle,
tirando per lo campo lor segnori,
e strascinando fegati[3] e budelle;
    e sonar[4] a raccolta trombatori[5]
e sufoli, flaùti e ciramelle
e tornar a le[6] schiere i feritori.

18. Sonetti de la semana: Mercoredie

    Ogni mercoredì corredo grande
di lepri, starne, fagian e paoni,[7]
e cotte manze ed[8] arrosti capponi
e quante son delicate vivande;
    donn'e[9] donzelle star per tutte bande,
figlie[10] di re, di conti e di baroni,
e donzellett'e[11] giovene[12] garzoni
servir portando amorose ghirlande;
    coppe, nappi, bacin d'oro e d'argento,
vin greco di rivèra[13] e di vernaccia,
frutta, confetti quanti li[14] è 'n[15] talento,
    e presentarvi uccellagioni[16] e caccia:

---

1 Caravaggi: "vedere andare."
2 Navone, Neri, Massèra, and Vitale: "vote." Caravaggi: "vuote."
3 Navone and Neri: "figati."
4 Caravaggi: "sonare."
5 Navone: "i trombatori."
6 Caravaggi: "tornare alle."
7 Navone: "fasani e pavoni." Caravaggi: "fagiani e paoni."
8 Navone and Neri: "et."
9 Navone, Neri, and Caravaggi: "donne e."
10 Navone: "figle."
11 Navone: "donzelletti."
12 Massèra and Vitale: "donzelletti gioveni." Neri: "donzellette gioven'e." Caravaggi: "donzellette e giovani."
13 Massèra, Vitale, and Caravaggi: "riviera."
14 Navone: "gli."
15 Neri: "in."
16 Navone: "uccellasoni."

and all the people there for conversation,
may they be happy and have a bright face.

19. Sonnets of the Week: Thursday

And every Thurday a tournament
and knights jousting, one against one,
and out in public, battles of fifty
against fifty, and hundred against hundred.
Armaments, chargers, and all equipment,
may everyone be supplied in equal measure;
from morning to evening, once their hunger's passed,
may everyone know exactly who won.
And then, to return home to their beloveds
where there'll be fine, superior beds,
and doctors will wrap their bruises and wounds,
and the ladies will help them with their hands;
and the young men will be so happy to see them
that they'll be healthy the following morning.

20. Sonnets of the Week: Friday

And every Friday, great ferocious hunts:
greyhounds, beagles, mastiffs, and hounds
and scrub forest, and miles of acres

e quanti son[1] a suo ragionamento[2]
sì sien allegri con[3] la chiara faccia.

19. Sonetti de la semana: Giovedie

Ed[4] ogni giovedì torneamento,[5]
e giostrar cavalier[6] ad uno ad uno,
e la battaglia sia 'n luogo[7] comuno,
a cinquanta e cinquanta, e cento e cento.
Arme, destrier[8] e tutto guarnimento,
sien d'un paraggio addobbati[9] ciascuno;
da terza a vespro, passato 'l digiuno,
allora si conosca chi ha[10] vénto.
E po'[11] tornar a casa a le lor vaghe,
ove serann'[12] i fin letti soprani;
e'[13] medici fasciar percosse e piaghe,
e le donne aitar con le lor mani:
e di vederle sì ciascun s'appaghe[14]
che la mattina[15] sien guariti e sani.

20. Sonetti de la semana: Venerdie

Ed[16] ogni venerdì gran caccia e forte:
veltri, bracchetti, mastin[17] e stivori,
e bosco basso miglia[18] di staiori,

---

1 Neri and Caravaggi: "sono."
2 Navone: "rasonamento."
3 Navone, Neri, Massèra, and Vitale: "sien allegri e con." Caravaggi: "sieno allegri e con."
4 Navone and Neri: "Et."
5 Navone and Neri: "torniamento." Caravaggi: "tornïamento."
6 Navone: "cavalieri."
7 Navone: "en logo." Neri: "en luogo."
8 Caravaggi: "destrieri."
9 Neri: "adobati."
10 Navone and Neri: "à."
11 Navone and Caravaggi: "poi."
12 Navone and Neri: "seran." Caravaggi: "seranno."
13 Navone, Neri, Massèra, and Vitale: "e."
14 Neri: "si paghi."
15 Navone and Neri: "matina."
16 Navone and Neri: "Et."
17 Navone and Caravaggi: "mastini."
18 Navone: "migla."

where many alert animals can be found;
the dogs can see clearly while tracking,
and the hunters are calling out commands;
the buglers trumpeting when the prey is caught,
and then many beasts are put to death.
And then to gather all the people and dogs
and say: "Send my love to her."
"By the Gospels, it will be a nice gift."
"It seems that our dogs have wings."
"Go, go, Belluccia, Picciuolo and Serpent,
because today's the day of a royal hunt!"

21. Sonnets of the Week: Saturday

And on Saturday, take pleasure and joy
in hawking and the flight of falcons,
and striking at cranes, and herons'
descents and ascents to great heights;
to wound geese with such force
that they lose their wings, thighs, and tails;
to spur on chargers and palfreys,

là 've[1] si troven molte bestie accorte,
    che possano veder, cacciando, scorte;
e rampognar[2] ensieme[3] i cacciatori,
cornando a caccia presa i cornatori:
ed[4] allor vegnan molte bestie morte.
    E po' recoglier[5] i cani e la gente,
e dicer: —L'amor[6] meo manda a cotale.
—A le[7] guagnèle, serà bel presente!
    —El[8] par ch'i nostri cani avesser ale!
—Tè tè, Belluccia, Picciuolo e Serpente,
ché oggi è 'l dì de la[9] caccia reale!

21. Sonetti de la semana: Sabato die

    E 'l sabato diletto ed allegrezza[10]
en[11] uccellar[12] e volar di falconi,
e percuotere grue, ed[13] alghironi
iscendere e salire 'n grand'altezza;[14]
    ed[15] a l'oche[16] ferir per tal fortezza[17]
che perdan l'ale, le cosce e'[18] gropponi;
corsier[19] e palafren mettere a sproni,

---

[1] Navone, Neri, and Caravaggi: "ove."

[2] Caravaggi: "rampognare."

[3] Massèra, Vitale, and Caravaggi: "insieme."

[4] Navone and Neri: "et."

[5] Navone: "po' recogler." Massèra and Vitale: "po' ricoglier." Caravaggi: "poi recogliere."

[6] Navone: "dicere: amor."

[7] Caravaggi: "Alle."

[8] Navone: "ei." Massèra and Vitale: "E'." Caravaggi: "Ei."

[9] Navone, Neri, and Caravaggi: "della."

[10] Navone: "El sabbato diletto et allegreza." Neri: "E 'l sabato diletto et alegrezza."

[11] Massèra, Vitale, and Caravaggi: "in."

[12] Caravaggi: "uccellare."

[13] Navone and Neri: "et."

[14] Navone: "e scendere e salire a grande alteza." Neri: "scendere e salire grand'altezza." Massèra and Vitale: "iscendere e salire grand'altezza." Caravaggi: "iscendere e salire in grand'altezza."

[15] Navone and Neri: "e."

[16] Caravaggi: "all'oche."

[17] Navone: "forteza."

[18] Navone: "le coscie e i."

[19] Navone and Caravaggi: "corsieri."

and shouts of glory and courage.
    And then, to return home and tell the cook,
"take these things and prepare them for tomorrow;
skin, cut, trim, and put them on the fire,
    and have fine wine and white bread,
and get ready for feasts and games:
make sure your kitchens aren't empty."

22. Sonnets of the Week: Sunday

    On the next day, at the break of
the coming day that's called Sunday,
whomever he likes best, damsel or lady,
many of them should be around him;
    in a colorful and adorned palace
to speak with the lady he loves the most;
may whichever thing she desires and yearns for
immediately be brought without delay.
    Dancing pageboys, knights in armor,
to search through Florence in every quarter,
piazzas, gardens, and green spaces;

ed isgridar[1] per gloria e per baldezza.[2]
    E po'[3] tornar a casa e dir al cuoco:
—To' queste cose e acconcia per dimane,
e pela, taglia,[4] assetta e metti a fòco;[5]
    ed abbie[6] fino vino e bianco pane,
ch'e'[7] s'apparecchia di far festa e giuoco;
fa'[8] che le tue cucine non sian[9] vane! —

22. Sonetti de la semana: Domenica die

    A la[10] domane, a l'apparér[11] del giorno
venente, che domenica si chiama,
qual più li[12] piace, damigella o dama,
abbiane molte che li sien da torno;[13]
    en[14] un palazzo dipinto[15] e adorno
ragionare[16] con quella che più ama;
qualunche cosa che desia e brama,
vegna in[17] presente senza far distorno.
    Danzar donzelli, armeggiar cavalieri,
cercar Fierenze[18] per ogni contrada,
per piazze, per giardin[19] e per verzieri;

---

1 Navone: "iscridar." Neri: "et iscridare."
2 Navone: "baldeza."
3 Caravaggi: "poi."
4 Navone: "tagla."
5 Massèra and Vitale: "a fuoco." Caravaggi: "a' fuoco."
6 Navone: "et abie." Neri: "e abie."
7 Navone: "ei."
8 Navone, Neri, and Caravaggi: "fa."
9 Neri: "sia." Caravaggi: "sien."
10 Caravaggi: "Alla."
11 Navone: "all'apparir." Neri and Vitale: "al parer." Caravaggi: "all'apparer."
12 Navone: "gli."
13 Navone: "abiane molte che gli sien dattorno." Neri: "abbiane molte che li sie da torno." Caravaggi: "abbiane molte che li sien d'attorno."
14 Massèra, Vitale, and Caravaggi: "in."
15 Navone and Neri: "depinto."
16 Navone: "rasonare."
17 Navone and Neri: "vegna en." Caravaggi: "venga in."
18 Neri, Massèra, Vitale, and Caravaggi: "Firenze."
19 Navone: "piaze, per giardini." Caravaggi: "piazze, per giardini."

and crowds on every street corner,
may all of them watch him eagerly;
and may every day go from good to better.

The Ceremonial Dressing of a Knight (Sonnets #23–27): The sole manuscript source for this *corona* states that it was supposed to consist of seventeen sonnets, but only five sonnets are extant.

23. The Ceremonial Dressing of a Knight: Introduction

Now we make a pageboy into a knight;
first, he needs to be remade as worthy
and mortgage his lands and castles
to acquire all the necessary items;
he gives tithes, bread, and wine to travelers,
beef, partridges, and capons as each likes,
pageboys and servants with perfect training,
bedrooms and beds, candles and torches;
and he should reflect on reined-in horses,
armorers and beautiful company,
standards and banners, horse coverings with bells,
and brigades with great baronies
guided by jongleurs through the lands,
ladies and damsels on every street.

e gente molta per ciascuna strada,
e tutti quanti li veggian volontieri:
ed[1] ogni dì de ben en[2] meglio[3] vada.

23. Vestimento del cavaliere: Introduzione

Ora si fa un donzello cavalieri:
e'[4] vuolsi far novellamente degno
e[5] pon sue terre e sue castell'a[6] pegno,
per ben fornirsi di ciò ch'è[7] mistieri;
annona, pane[8] e vin dà a' forestieri,
manze, pernici[9] e cappon per ingegno;
donzelli e servidori a dritto segno,
camere e letta,[10] cerotti e doppieri;
e pens'a[11] molti affrenati cavagli,
armeggiatori e bella compagnia,
aste e bandiere,[12] coverte e sonagli
ed istormenti con gran baronia,
e[13] giucolar per la terra guidàgli,
donne e donzelle per ciascuna via!

---

1 Navone and Neri: "et."
2 Massèra, Vitale, and Caravaggi: "di bene in."
3 Navone: "meglo."
4 Navone, Neri, Massèra, and Vitale: "e."
5 Navone, Neri, Massèra, and Vitale: "e'."
6 Navone: "castella a."
7 Navone: "k'è."
8 Neri: "e pane."
9 Neri: "e pernici."
10 Navone: "chamere elette." Neri, Massèra, and Vitale: "camere elette."
11 Navone: "pensa a." Massèra and Vitale: "pens'a'."
12 Navone and Caravaggi: "aste, bandiere."
13 Massèra and Vitale: "e'."

24. The Ceremonial Dressing of a Knight: Prowess

Here's Prowess, who undresses him quickly
and says: "Friend, you need to change
because I like to see men naked,
and I want you to know I want nothing else.
And leave behind every habit you're used to,
and struggle and sweat right away;
if you do this, you'll be one of my lovers
so that you won't regret or feel pain to do good."
And when she sees his unclothed body,
she immediately takes him into her arms
saying, "You've offered your flesh to me.
I accept it, and make this gift to you
so that you'll be sure in your works:
I won't ever be quiet about your good deeds."

25. The Ceremonial Dressing of a Knight: Humility

Humility sweetly receives him
and says: "I want nothing to soil you,
so I now need to clean and bathe you
and I'll make you whiter than snow.
Now understand what I'll say briefly:
I want to carry the keys to your heart,

24. Vestimento del cavaliere: Prodezza

Ecco[1] Prodezza,[2] che tosto lo spoglia
e dice: —Amico,[3] e' convien che tu mudi,
per ciò ch'i' vo' veder li uomini nudi,
e vo' che sappi non abbo altra voglia.
E lascia ogni costume che far soglia,
e nuovamente t'affatichi e sudi;
se questo fai, tu sarai de' miei drudi,
pur che ben far non t'incresca[4] né doglia. —
E quando vede le membra scoperte,[5]
immantenente se le[6] reca in braccio,
dicendo: —Queste carni[7] m'hai[8] offerte;
i' le[9] ricevo e questo don ti faccio,
acciò che[10] le tue opere sien certe:
che[11] ogni tuo ben far già mai[12] non taccio. —

25. Vestimento del cavaliere: Umiltà

Umiltà[13] dolcemente il riceve
e dice: —Punto non vo' che ti[14] gravi,
ch'e'[15] pur convèn[16] ch'io ti rimondi e lavi,
e farotti più bianco che la neve.
E 'ntendi[17] quel ched io ti dico breve:
ch'i'[18] vo' portar de lo[19] tuo cor le chiavi

---

1 Navone: "Eccho."
2 Neri: "prodezza."
3 Navone: "amicho."
4 Navone: "increscha."
5 Navone: "schoperte."
6 Neri: "sì le."
7 Navone: "charni."
8 Neri: "m'ài."
9 Navone, Massèra, and Vitale: "te."
10 Navone: "ke."
11 Massèra: "ché."
12 Navone: "giammai."
13 Navone: "Humiltà."
14 Navone: "tti."
15 Navone and Neri: "che." Massèra: "ché."
16 Navone: "chonven." Neri: "conven." Caravaggi: "convien."
17 Navone: "Entendi." Neri: "Entende." Caravaggi: "e intendi."
18 Navone: "k'i'."
19 Caravaggi: "dello."

and you'll need to sail in my manner
and I'll guide you as if you were me.
    But you'll need to drive one thing away;
you know that Pride is my enemy
so it can no longer reside within you.
    I'll become such a friend to you
that everyone will find it pleasing;
whoever is nourished by me behaves thus."

26. The Ceremonial Dressing of a Knight: Discretion

    Discretion arrives immediately
and dries him with a bright, lovely cloth,
and quickly puts him in her bed
with linen and silk, coverlets and feathers.
    Now consider this: she kept him there till day
with singing, with music, and with pleasures!
To perfect him she accompanied him
with young knights, which was appropriate.
    Then she said: "Rise up right away
because you need to be reborn into the world;
keep in mind the orders you are now taking."

ed[1] a mio modo converrà[2] che navi,
ed[3] io ti guiderò sì come meve.
    Ma d'una cosa[4] far tosto ti spaccia,
ché[5] tu sai che soperbia m'è nimica:[6]
che più con teco dimoro[7] non faccia.
    I' ti sarabbo[8] così fatta amica,[9]
ch'e'[10] converrà ch'a tutta gente piaccia;
e così fa chi di me si notrica. —[11]

26. Vestimento del cavaliere: Discrezïone

    Discrezïone incontanente venne
e sì l'asciuga d'un bel drappo e netto,
e tostamente sì 'l mette 'n[12] sul[13] letto
di lin, di seta, coverture[14] e penne.
    Or ti ripensa: enfin[15] al dì 'l vi[16] tenne
con canti, con sonare e con diletto!
Accompagnollo, per farlo perfetto,
di novi[17] cavalier, che ben s'avvenne.
    Poi disse: —Lieva suso immantenente,
ch'e'[18] ti convien rinascere nel mondo,
e l'ordine che prendi tieni a mente. —

[1] Navone and Neri: "et."
[2] Navone: "chonverrà."
[3] Navone and Neri: "et."
[4] Navone: "Mad una chosa."
[5] Neri: "che."
[6] Navone: "nimicha."
[7] Neri: "dimora."
[8] Neri: "sarebbo."
[9] Navone: "amicha."
[10] Navone, Neri, and Massèra: "che."
[11] Navone: "notricha."
[12] Caravaggi: "in."
[13] Neri: "su 'l."
[14] Navone: "choverture."
[15] Massèra and Vitale: "e 'nfin." Caravaggi: "infino."
[16] Navone, Neri, and Caravaggi: "vi 'l."
[17] Neri and Caravaggi: "nuovi."
[18] Navone: "che." Massèra and Vitale: "ché."

He has such deep thoughts—there's no bottom to them—
about the bond he wants to take on
and he can't say, "I hide myself from this."

27. The Ceremonial Dressing of a Knight: Gaiety

Gaiety arrives, with lightheartedness and feasts,
all florid so that she appears a rose garden;
she wears beautiful vestments made
of linen, of silk, of velvet and ermine;
a headcloth, a hood with a garland on her head,
and so adorned that she resembles May,
with so many people that the balcony trembles;
and she makes all work in you manifest.
She has him stand straight in hose, and slippers,
a purse, a belt decorated with silver,
which are worn beneath his leather garments.
With singing and every instrument playing,
she shows him to the ladies and damsels
and everyone present in the assembly.

Sonnets (#28–32): Folgore's remaining sonnets deal primarily with political and social themes. He describes the internecine warfare between Pisa's Ghibellines (the pro-emperor party) against the pro-pope Guelphs of San Gimignano and much of Tuscany. He insults as pallid cowards the Ghibellines of Pisa, whose emblem is the Hare. He decries the Ghibelline victory in Montecatini (1315), which resulted in the loss of the Guelph castles, San Martino, Altopascio, and San Michele to the Ghibellines, and the despoiling of the cathedral of San Frediano. He also castigates the leader of Italy's Guelphs, King Roberto II of Naples, for his lukewarm support, and he compares the spineless Guelphs to two great examples of treason: Ganelon, the betrayer of Roland, and the Battle of Ceprano, where Frederick II's son Manfred, was defeated when his subjects in Apulia betrayed him to Charles I ("the Apulian"). Dante recalls the latter event in *Inferno* 28: 17: "at Ceperano, where every Apulian was a liar."[1]

[1] Cited from Dante Alighieri, *The Divine Comedy of Dante Alighieri: Inferno*, ed. and trans., Robert M. Durling (New York, Oxford: Oxford University Press, 1996).

Egli ha tanti pensier, che non ha[1] fondo,
del gran legame dov'entrar si sente;
e non può dir: —A questo mi nascondo. —[2]

27. Vestimento del cavaliere: Allegrezza

Giugne[3] Allegrezza[4] con letizia e festa,
tutta[5] fiorita che pare un rosaio;
di lin, di seta, di drappo e di vaio
allor li porta bellissima vesta,
vetta, cappuccio con ghirlanda 'n[6] testa,
e sì adorno l'ha che[7] pare un maio:
con tanta gente che trema 'l[8] solaio;
allor sì[9] fece l'opra manifesta.
E ritto l'ha[10] in calze ed[11] in pianelle,
borsa, cintura inorata d'argento,
che[12] stanno sotto la leggiadra pelle;
cantar, sonando ciascuno stormento,
mostrando lui a donne ed[13] a donzelle
e quanti sono a questo assembramento.

---

[1] Neri: "à."
[2] Navone: "naschondo."
[3] Caravaggi: "Giunge."
[4] Neri: "allegrezza."
[5] Navone: "tucta."
[6] Caravaggi: "in."
[7] Navone: "l'à ke." Neri: "l'à che."
[8] Caravaggi: "il."
[9] Massèra and Vitale: "si."
[10] Navone and Neri: "l'à."
[11] Navone and Neri: "et."
[12] Navone: "ke."
[13] Navone and Neri: "et."

Sonnets

28.

You are all whiter than ermine,
you counts, knights, and pageboys of Pisa,
and through careful study of your hats,
you think you can outdo the Florentines;
and you make the Ghibellines be faithful
everywhere, in cities or in their castles.
When I see you all so brave and able
beneath your armor, you look like paladins.
You're always courageous, like hunted hares,
when you confront the Genoese on the sea,
and you can't face the Lucchese people;
and just as dogs with bones become gentle,
so may Folgore get something he likes:
may you set yourselves against all foreigners.

29.

I don't praise you, God, and I don't adore you,
and I don't pray to you, and I don't thank you,
and I don't serve you; but I am happier
than the souls that go to purgatory

Sonetti

28.

Più lichisati siete ch'ermellini,
conti[1] pisan, cavalieri e donzelli,
e per istudio de' vostri cappelli
credete vantaggiare[2] i fiorentini;
e franchi fate stare i ghibellini
in ogni parte, o cittadi o castelli:[3]
veggendovi[4] sì osi e sì isnelli
sotto l'arme, parete paladini.
Valentri[5] sempre come lepre in caccia
a riscontrare[6] in mare i genovesi,[7]
e co'[8] lucchesi non avete faccia;
e come i can[9] de l'ossa[10] son cortesi,[11]
se Folgore abbia cosa[12] che gli piaccia,
siate voi contro[13] a tutti li foresi.

29.

Eo[14] non ti lodo, Dio, e non ti adoro
e non ti prego, e non ti rengrazio,[15]
e non ti servo: ch'eo ne so'[16] più sazio
che l'anime[17] di stare 'n[18] purgatoro:

---

[1] Navone: "chonti."
[2] Navone: "chredete vantagiare."
[3] Navone: "chastelli."
[4] Navone: "vegiendovi."
[5] Navone, Neri, Massèra, Vitale, and Caravaggi: "Valenti."
[6] Navone: "rischontrare."
[7] Navone: "gienovesi."
[8] Navone: "cho'."
[9] Navone: "chome i chan."
[10] Caravaggi: "dell'ossa."
[11] Navone: "chortesi."
[12] Navone: "Folghore abia chosa."
[13] Navone: "chontro."
[14] Massèra and Vitale: "Io."
[15] Massèra and Vitale: "ringrazio."
[16] Navone, Neri, and Caravaggi: "ch'eo ne son." Massèra: "ch'io ne so'." Vitale: "ch'io ne so."
[17] Navone and Neri: "l'aneme."
[18] Neri: "star en." Caravaggi: "in."

because you've put the Guelphs to such torment
that the Ghibellines deride and torture them;
and if Uguccione demanded a toll from you
you would pay it without any delay.
And they certainly know you so very well —
they took San Martin and Altopasso from you,
and San Michele, and the treasure you lost.
And you've made that rotten people so fat
that out of pride they'll demand tribute from you,
and you've changed your heart so that it seems a stone.

30.

Guelphs, since you shielded your backsides
and since you struck so hard with your spurs
while keeping the reins toward home,
you've made lions out of rabbits.
Now your man is dying in those evil lands,
which he would have won if you'd thrust the pikes;
you've made falcons out of owls,
so that it seems that mere wind carries and drives you.
But I suggest that you comport yourselves
like the esteemed King Roberto

per che tu hai mess'i[1] guelfi a tal martòro,
ch'i' ghibellini ne fan beffe e strazio;
e se Uguccion ti comandasse il dazio,
tu 'l pagaresti senza perentoro.[2]
Ed hanti[3] certo sì ben conosciuto,
tolto t'han[4] San Martin[5] ed[6] Altopasso
e San Michel[7] e 'l tesoro[8] c'hai[9] perduto;
e[10] hai[11] quel popol marcio[12] così grasso,
che per soperbia[13] cherranti[14] 'l tributo:
e tu hai[15] fatto 'l cor che par d'un sasso.

30.

Guelfi, per fare scudo de le[16] reni
avete fatti i conigli leoni,
e per ferir sì forte di speroni
tenendo vòlti verso casa i freni.
E tal perisce en[17] malvagi[18] terreni,
che vincerebbe a dar con li[19] spontoni;[20]
fatto avete le pùpule falconi,
sì par che 'l vento ve ne porti e meni.
Però vi do conseglio che facciate
di quelle del pregiato[21] re Roberto:

---

1 Navone and Caravaggi: "perché tu hai messi i." Neri: "perché tu ài messi i."
2 Navone: "peremptoro."
3 Navone: "Er' anti." Neri: "Et ànti."
4 Navone: "t'ha 'n." Neri: "t'àn."
5 Caravaggi: "Martino."
6 Neri: "et."
7 Caravaggi: "Michele."
8 Neri and Caravaggi: "tesor."
9 Neri: "ch'ài."
10 Caravaggi: "ed."
11 Neri: "ài."
12 Navone, Neri, Massèra, and Vitale: "marzo."
13 Neri: "soperba." Massèra and Vitale: "superbia."
14 Navone: "cher' anti."
15 Neri: "ài."
16 Caravaggi: "delle."
17 Neri: "'n." Massèra, Vitale, and Caravaggi: "in."
18 Navone: "malvasi."
19 Navone, Neri, and Caravaggi: "gli."
20 Massèra and Vitale: "spuntoni."
21 Navone: "presiato."

and you confess your sins, and forgive.
He made peace with Pisa, this is certain:
he doesn't care about the accursed flesh
that was left in the wilderness for the wolves.

31.

If you thus waged war or sued for peace,
Guelphs, just like how you create factions.
Because not even a trace of reason reigns in you;
evil still grows and goodness dies off silently.
One man watches and dislikes the other's
being and status and condition;
the Apulian and Ganelon reign among you,
and everyone blows air on the harsh fire.
Don't you remember Montecatini,
how the wives and the mothers suffered
widowhood thanks to the Ghibellines?
And fathers, brothers, sons, and relatives,
and whoever loved well his neighbors
would still do combat with clenched teeth.

e rendetevi en[1] colpa e perdonate.
Con Pisa ha[2] fatto pace, quest'è[3] certo;
non cura de le[4] carni malfatate,[5]
che son remase[6] a' lupi in quel deserto.

31.

Così faceste voi o guerra o pace,
guelfi, sì come siete en devisione,[7]
ché 'n[8] voi non[9] regna ponto[10] di[11] ragione,[12]
lo mal pur cresce e 'l ben s'ammorta e tace.
E l'uno contra l'altro isguarda e spiace
lo suo[13] essere e stato e condizione;
fra voi regna il pugliese e 'l Ganelone
e ciascun soffia nel fòco[14] penace.
Non vi recorda[15] di Montecatini,
come le mogli e le madri[16] dolenti
fan vedovaggio per gli[17] ghibellini?
E babbi, frati, figliuoli[18] e parenti
e chi amasse bene i soi[19] vicini
combatterebbe ancora a stretti denti!

---

1 Massèra, Vitale, and Caravaggi: "in."
2 Navone and Neri: "à."
3 Navone: "questo è."
4 Caravaggi: "delle."
5 Navone: "mal fatate."
6 Massèra and Vitale: "rimase."
7 Massèra and Vitale: "in divisione."
8 Navone: "ch'en." Caravaggi: "ché in."
9 Neri: "no."
10 Neri, Massèra, and Vitale: "punto."
11 Neri: "de."
12 Navone: "rasone."
13 Navone and Neri: "suo."
14 Massèra, Vitale, and Caravaggi: "fuoco."
15 Neri, Massèra, Vitale, and Caravaggi: "ricorda."
16 Navone and Neri: "madre."
17 Neri: "li."
18 Navone: "figloli." Neri: "figlioli."
19 Navone, Neri, Massèra, Vitale, and Caravaggi: "suoi."

32.

I call, "Courtesy, courtesy, courtesy,"
but no one answers me anywhere,
and whoever should show courtesy hides it;
for this reason, whoever should, lives cheaply.
People have bitten the hook of avarice,
and it destroys and confuses all graces.
But if I feel pain, I also know why:
I call out to God about you, lords.
Because you've taken Courtesy, my mother,
and put her under a foot that doesn't lift up;
she's stuck there, but you're able to move on.
We're all descendents of Adam and Eve;
even though you can, you don't give or spend:
whoever raises his children thus has an evil nature.

32.

Cortesia cortesia cortesia chiamo
e da nessuna parte mi risponde,[1]
e chi la dée mostrar sì la nasconde,
e per ciò a cui besogna[2] vive gramo.
Avarizia[3] le gente[4] ha[5] prese a l'amo,[6]
ed[7] ogne[8] grazia distrugge[9] e confonde:
però se eo me[10] doglio,[11] eo[12] so ben onde;
de voi, possente,[13] a Deo me ne richiamo.[14]
Ché la mia madre cortesia avete
messa sì sotto 'l[15] piè che non si leva;
l'aver ci sta, voi non ci rimanete;[16]
tutti sièm nati di Adamo[17] e di Eva;
potendo, non donate e non spendete:
mal ha natura chi ai[18] figli alleva.

---

[1] Navone and Neri: "responde."
[2] Neri, Massèra, Vitale, and Caravaggi: "bisogna."
[3] Navone and Neri: "avaricia."
[4] Massèra, Vitale, and Caravaggi: "genti."
[5] Neri: "à."
[6] Navone and Caravaggi: "all'amo."
[7] Navone and Neri: "et."
[8] Massèra, Vitale, and Caravaggi: "ogni."
[9] Navone: "destrugge."
[10] Caravaggi: "mi."
[11] Navone: "doglo."
[12] Massèra and Vitale: "s'io me ne doglio, io."
[13] Massèra, Vitale, and Caravaggi: "di voi, possenti."
[14] Navone and Neri: "reclamo."
[15] Caravaggi: "il."
[16] Navone and Neri: "remanete."
[17] Navone, Neri, Massèra, and Vitale: "Adam."
[18] Navone: "Mal' a nadura chi tai." Neri: "Mal'à natura chi tai." Massèra, Vitale, and Caravaggi: "mal'ha natura chi tai."

Sonnets of debated attribution (#33–35)[1]

33.

Dear friend, not all plants will flower,
nor every flower that appears brings forth fruit;
and not every word is virtuous,
nor does every stone that exists have power;
and some things that seem unripe are mature
and some things seem painful but are comforts;
every candle that you see is not bright:
some have flames but appear lifeless.
But it's necessary for a wise man
not to bundle up all types of herb,
not to load each rock on his back,
nor to try out every suggestion,
nor to walk alongside all people:
I wasn't moved to say this without reason.

[1] The three sonnets of dubious attribution are not found in the editions by Massèra and Vitale. Navone and Neri considered this sonnet and the following to be among Folgore's authentic poems.

Sonetti dubbi

33.

Amico caro, non fiorisce ogni[1] erba,
né ogni[2] fior che par, frutto non porta;
e non è vertudiosa,[3] ogne[4] verba,
né ha[5] vertù ogne[6] pietra[7] ch'è orta;
e tal cosa è matura e pare[8] acerba,
e tal se par doler che se conforta;
ogne[9] cèra[10] che par, non è soperba,[11]
cosa è che getta fiamma e che par morta.
Però non se convèn[12] ad omo[13] saggio
voler adesso far d'ogn'erba fasso,
né d'ogne[14] petra carecarsi[15] 'l dosso,
né voler trar di ogni[16] parola saggio,
né con tutta la gente andare[17] a passo;
senza ragion[18] a dir ciò non[19] son mosso.

---

[1] Navone: "ogne."
[2] Navone: "ogne."
[3] Navone and Neri: "virtuosa."
[4] Caravaggi: "ogni."
[5] Neri: "à."
[6] Caravaggi: "ogni."
[7] Navone: "virtù ogne pedra."
[8] Navone: "tal'."
[9] Caravaggi: "ogni"
[10] Navone: "ciera."
[11] Neri: "superba."
[12] Caravaggi: "convien."
[13] Navone: "homo." Caravaggi: "uomo."
[14] Caravaggi: "ogni."
[15] Navone: "pedra caricarsi." Neri: "petra caricarsi." Caravaggi: "pietra caricarsi."
[16] Neri: "de ogni." Caravaggi: "d'ogni."
[17] Navone and Neri: "andar."
[18] Navone: "rason."
[19] Navone: "eo non."

34.

When desire so rules over a man,
that reason has no power or space,
often he will laugh about his tears
and will make jokes about his grave pains;
and he would be deprived of all good wisdom
if he judged fire to be as cold as snow;
similarly, those men display joys and sing
about that which should cause them suffering.
But he should feel the deepest heartache
who submits his reason to desire,
and follows his yearnings without restraint;
for there is no wealthier lordship
than to maintain oneself righteously,
to pursue honor and to flee vanity.

34.

Quando la voglia[1] segnoreggia tanto,
che la ragion non ha poter né[2] loco,
ispesse[3] volte ride l'om[4] di pianto
e de[5] grave doglienza mostra[6] gioco;
e ben seria[7] de bon[8] savere affranto
chi fredda neve giudicasse fòco;
simil son que'[9], che gioi' mostrano[10] e canto
de[11] quel,[12] onde doler devrian[13] un poco.
Ma ben se pò coralmente dolere
chi sommette ragion[14] a voluntade[15]
e segue senza freno su'[16] volere;
che non è già sì ricca podestade
com'[17] se medesmo a dritto mantenere,
seguire[18] pregio,[19] fùgger vanitade.

---

1 Navone: "vogla."
2 Navone: "rason non a poder in." Neri: "ragion non à poter in."
3 Navone and Neri: "spesse."
4 Navone: "l'omo." Neri and Caravaggi: "l'uom."
5 Caravaggi: "di."
6 Navone: "dolenza monstra."
7 Navone: "saria."
8 Caravaggi: "di buon."
9 Navone and Neri: "quelli."
10 Navone: "monstra." Neri: "mostra."
11 Caravaggi: "di."
12 Navone and Neri: "quell'."
13 Navone and Neri: "devria."
14 Caravaggi: "ragione."
15 Navone: "volontade."
16 Navone and Caravaggi: "suo." Neri: "sò."
17 Navone and Neri: "com."
18 Neri: "e seguir."
19 Navone: "presio."

35.

The flower of virtue is noble courage,
and the fruit of virtue is honor;
the vase of virtue is valor,
and the name of virtue is wise man;
the mirror of virtue sees no outrage,
and the face of virtue, bright color;
the love of virtue is a good servant,
and the gift of virtue is sweet lineage;
the bed of virtue is knowledge,
and the seat of virtue, loyal love;
the power of virtue is patience,
the work of virtue, to be loyal;
the arm of virtue is lovely welcome.
All virtue is returning good for ill.

35.[1]

Fior di virtù sì è gentil coraggio
e frutto di virtù sì è onore,
e vaso di virtù sì è valore
e nome di virtù è uomo saggio;
e specchio di virtù non vede oltraggio
e viso di virtù, chiaro colore,
ed amor di virtù, buon servitore,
e dono di virtù, dolce lignaggio.
E letto di virtù è conoscenza,
e seggio di virtù, amor leale,
e poder di virtù è sofferenza;
e opera di virtù, esser leale,
e braccio di virtù, bella accoglienza:
tutta virtù è render ben per male.

[1] Only Caravaggi's edition contains this sonnet.

Chapter Two:
Cenne da la Chitarra
(d. 1334)

Sonnets of the Months: A line-by-line parody of Folgore's sonnets of the months. Each sonnet employs the same rhyme scheme as the corresponding poem in Folgore's *corona*. Cenne replaces Folgore's pleasant items with annoyances, and overturns Folgore's courtly values with their juxtaposed vices. Similarly, the *corona* is addressed to a group of youths, this time led by Paglierino, and including Benci, Lippo da Chianciano, and Senso da Panical; nothing is currently known about any of these men. However, at the end of the sonnet to September, Cenne criticizes the Salimbeni family, the apparent recipients of Folgore's *corona*, suggesting a political basis for his satire.

1. Sonnets of the Months: Introduction

To the cheap company without any gear,
in all those parts wherever they may be,[1]
I put them before dice and game tables
so that they'll all be laid out in the sun;[2]
and so they'll be in undershirts every month
to go about lightly, seeking forgiveness;
among the slime and mud I imprison them,
and I'll tame them with differing weights.
And may Paglierino be their captain
and may he pay part of their tavern bill,
with Benci and wise Lippo from Chianciano,
and Senso da Panical, who trots lightly:
whoever saw him defend himself down on the plain
would all say: "He looks like a duckling!"

[1] Cenne's opening verses parallel those found in Folgore's introductory sonnet, substituting poverty for nobility and courteousness.

[2] That is to say, their gambling will result in the loss of clothing. See Cowell, *At Play in the Tavern: Signs, Coins and Bodies in the Middle Ages*, 6–8.

1. Sonetti de' Mesi: Introduzione

A la[1] brigata avara senza arnese:[2]
in tutte quelle parti dove sono,
davanti a' dadi e tavolier li pono,
perché al sole stien tutti distese;[3]
ed[4] in camicia stieno[5] tutti i mese[6]
per poter più legger[7] ire al perdono:
entro la malta e 'l fango gl'[8] imprigiono,
e sien domati con diversi pese.[9]
E Paglierino sia lor capitano;
e[10] abbia[11] parte di tutto lo scotto,
con Benci e Lippo savio da Chianciano,[12]
Senso da Panical, c'ha legger[13] trotto:
chi lo vedesse schermir giuso al piano,
ciascun direbbe: — E' pare un anitrotto! —

---

1 Neri: "Alla."
2 Navone, Neri, Massèra, and Vitale: "arnesi."
3 Navone, Neri, Massèra, and Vitale: "distesi."
4 Navone and Neri: "e."
5 Navone, Massèra, and Vitale: "stiano."
6 Navone, Neri, Massèra, andVitale: "mesi."
7 Navone and Neri: "leggier."
8 Navone: "gli."
9 Navone, Neri, Massèra, and Vitale: "pesi."
10 Massèra and Vitale: "ed."
11 Navone: "habbia."
12 Navone, Neri, and Massèra: "Chianzano."
13 Navone: "ch'ha leggier." Neri: "ch'à leggier."

2. Sonnets of the Months: January

I give you in the month of January
courts filled with smoke, like mountain men's huts,
beds[1] like the Genoese have at sea,
water and wind that never dies down;
poor servant girls by the bushelful;
for drinking, strong Calabrian vinegar;
like ribalds,[2] always wearing riding gear
and tattered clothes, without any money.
And I give you such a residence
with a dark, old woman, angry and deformed,[3]
with everyone tossing snow around;
seated on a rough bench near to you,
and admiring the woman's adorned face,
so may the needy crew take repose.

3. Sonnets of the Months: February

In February I put you in an icy valley
with large, old bears from the mountains,
and you hunting in tattered leggings,
with the snow falling and then melting;

[1] The first three lines of Cenne's January sonnet parallel those found in Folgore's poem, replacing the warmth and brightness of Folgore's courts with smoke and poverty.

[2] Italian statutes defined the ribald as someone who undressed down to his underclothes while gambling; as an insult, it indicated someone for whom gambling and prostitution were central to identity. See Richard C. Trexler, "Correre la Terra: Collective Insults in the Late Middle Ages," in *Dependence in Context in Renaissance Florence* (Binghamton NY: Medieval & Renaissance Texts and Studies, 1994): 113–70, at 116–21.

[3] Cenne evokes the image of the malformed, sunburnt peasant with this old woman. See Paul Freedman, *Images of the Medieval Peasant,* 139–40.

2. Sonetti de' Mesi: Di gennaio

Io vi doto, del mese de[1] gennaio
corti con fumo al modo montanese,
letta qual ha[2] nel mare il genovese,
acqua, e vento[3] che non cali maio;
povertà di[4] fanciulle[5] a colmo staio;
da ber, aceto forte galavrese:
come rubaldi star sempre in arnese,[6]
con panni rotti senza alcun denaio.
Ancor vi do così fatto soggiorno,
con una veglia[7] nera, vizza e ranca,[8]
catuno gittando la neve[9] a torno;
appresso a voi[10] seder in una banca,[11]
e resmirando[12] quel suo[13] viso adorno,
così riposi[14] la brigata manca.[15]

3. Sonetti de' Mesi: Di febbraio

Di febbraio[16] vi metto in valle ghiaccia
con orsi grandi vegli montanari,
e voi cacciando con rotti calzari,
la nieve[17] metta sempre e si[18] disfaccia;

[1] Massèra and Vitale: "di."

[2] Navone: "quali à." Neri: "qual'à."

[3] Navone: "aqua e vento." Vitale: "acqua con vento."

[4] Navone: "en."

[5] Neri: "povertà, fanciulli."

[6] Navone and Neri: "e star come ribaldo en arnese." Massèra and Vitale: "e stare come ribaldo in arnese."

[7] Navone: "vegla."

[8] Navone: "rancha."

[9] Navone: "ciascuno gittando la neve." Neri, Massèra, and Vitale: "catun gittando de la neve."

[10] Navone, Neri, Massèra, and Vitale: "appresso voi."

[11] Navone: "bancha."

[12] Massèra and Vitale: "rismirando."

[13] Neri: "so'."

[14] Navone and Neri: "reposi."

[15] Navone: "mancha."

[16] Navone and Neri: "febraio."

[17] Neri, Massèra, and Vitale: "neve."

[18] Navone: "mai."

and what one person likes, the other doesn't;
with reluctant squires and stable boys;
returning to the stingy tavern-keepers,
their wives weaving cloths and spinning yarn.
And I want you to be without lovers,
with apple wine that turns your stomach,
and in the hotels, great sighs and weeping;
earthquakes and winds—but without damage.
They should be strong enough to scare everyone
from early evening until the morning.

4. Sonnets of the Months: March

In March I have you rest in this way:
on Apulian plains among many lakes,
and in them many leeches and frogs,
and may you have plums and pears to eat,
rancid old nut oil, mornings and evenings,
to make fritters; orange trees and cedars;
many rowboats with oars and rudders,
but may you not be able to leave the banks!

e quel che piace a l'uno, a l'altro spiaccia:
con fanti ben retrosi e bacalari;[1]
tornando poi la sera ad osti cari,[2]
lor moglie[3] tesser tele ed[4] ordir accia.
E' n[5] questo vo' che siate senz'amanti,[6]
con vin di pome che 'l stomaco[7] affina;
in tal[8] alberghi gran sospiri e pianti,
tremoti, venti: e non sian[9] con ruina,
ma sian sì forte, che ciascun si smanti[10]
da prima sera infino la mattina.[11]

4. Sonetti de' Mesi: Di marzo

Di marzo vi riposo en tal manèra,[12]
en[13] Puglia[14] piana, tra molti lagoni,
e 'n essi[15] gran mignatte e ranaglioni;[16]
poi da mangiar abbiate[17] sorbe e pera,
oleo de[18] noce veglio,[19] mane e sera,
per far caldegli; arance[20] e gran cidroni,
barchette assai con remi e con timoni;
ma'[21] non possiate uscir de tal rivèra.[22]

---

1 Navone: "bachalari."
2 Navone: "chari."
3 Navone: "mogle." Neri: "mogli."
4 Navone and Neri: "et."
5 Navone: "En."
6 Navone, Neri, Massèra, and Vitale: "senza manti."
7 Navone: "ch'el stomago." Neri: "che 'l stomago."
8 Navone: "tali."
9 Navone: "nosia." Neri: "no sia."
10 Navone, Neri, Massèra, and Vitale: "stanchi."
11 Navone: "enfino la matina." Neri: "in fino la mattina."
12 Massèra and Vitale: "maniera."
13 Massèra and Vitale: "in."
14 Navone: "Pugla."
15 Navone: "en esse." Neri: "e 'n esse."
16 Navone: "ranagloni."
17 Navone: "abiate."
18 Navone, Massèra, and Vitale: "di."
19 Navone: "veglo."
20 Navone: "calde gli arance."
21 Navone, Neri, Massèra, and Vitale: "ma."
22 Massèra and Vitale: "riviera."

Straw huts with many olive trees;
to drink, spoiled wine that's truly black;
beds made of cattails, and pillows stuffed with reeds.
Among you, lords, may there be a fierce priest
who never absolves you of any sins—
and may there be monasteries everywhere![1]

5. Sonnets of the Months: April

In April I give you a life without complaints:
swarms of horseflies and herds of donkeys
braying so loudly that it no longer bothers you—
as many as are in Perugia or Bevagna;
with Romagnole henchmen from the country
and all of them crowded together throwing punches;
and when they finally tire of this game,
they're replaced with farmhands from the Romagna plain.
As dancers, I give you old Armenians;[2]
a bell that resounds horribly:
may there be rustling for you that never gets better!
And whoever shows off by giving widely,
may his neighbors all around get angry with him,
because they speak about such good people!

---

[1] Folgore concludes his March sonnet by wishing that the company should not be bothered by the rantings of priests, and should be distant from monasteries. In contrast, Cenne hopes for a stern priest and, further, monasteries everywhere.

[2] Cenne writes the second quatrain in parallel to that of Folgore's April sonnet. In contrast to Folgore's elegant singers and dancers, trained in France and Provence, Cenne posits rustic henchmen and farmers.

Case de[1] paglia[2] con diversi razzi;[3]
da bere vin cercon[4] che sia ben nero;
letta di schiance[5] e di gionchi piumazzi.[6]
Tra voi, signori,[7] sia un priete fèro,
che da nessun peccato vi dislazzi;
per ciascun luogo v'abbia un munistero.[8]

5. Sonetti de' Mesi: Di aprile

Di aprile vi do vita senza lagna:
tavàni a schiera con asene[9] a tresca,
ragghiando[10] forte per che[11] non v'incresca,
quanti ne sono in Perósa o Bevagna;
con birri romaneschi di campagna,
e ciascadun di pugna sì vi mesca:
e quando questo a gioco[12] non riesca,
restori[13] i marri de' pian de Romagna.
Per danzatori vi do vegli armini;
una campana,[14] la qual peggio sòna,[15]
stormento sia a voi e non refini.[16]
E quel che 'n millantar sì largo dona,
en[17] ira vegna de li soi[18] vicini,
per che di cotal gente sì ragiona.

---

1 Massèra and Vitale: "di."
2 Navone: "pagla."
3 Navone: "raggi."
4 Navone, Neri, Massèra, and Vitale: "gergon."
5 Neri, Massèra, and Vitale: "schianze."
6 Navone: "piumacci."
7 Neri: "signor."
8 Navone: "loco v'abia un monastero." Neri: "loco v'abbia un monistero."
9 Navone and Neri: "aseni." Massèra and Vitale: "asini."
10 Navone and Neri: "raiando."
11 Navone and Neri: "perché."
12 Navone: "questo fatto." Neri: "quest'è a ciò che."
13 Massèra and Vitale: "ristori."
14 Navone: "compagna."
15 Massèra and Vitale: "suona."
16 Massèra and Vitale: "rifini."
17 Massèra and Vitale: "in."
18 Navone, Massèra, and Vitale: "suoi."

6. Sonnets of the Months: May

For May I want you to have jousts
against people who are laborers,
with mules and big, limping chargers,
and with braided garlic as breast plates.
And may there be great dances around you
by the unkempt, shouting peasantry,
who emanate such great perspiration
that it twirls in the air and never subsides.
And then may other peasants present you
with leek-like onions and with chestnuts,
jumping for joy and giving speeches.
Manure below, and pitchforks above;
farmers and old women kissing each others' cheeks,
and conversations about sheep and pigs.[1]

7. Sonnets of the Months: June

In June, may you be in the countryside
where there are crows and herons;
swamps all around you, but no sailboats,
and in the middle, may there be a small island,

[1] Cenne closely structures his May sonnet around Folgore's poem, which also portrays a joust. Folgore presents the noble steeds of the valiant warriors (vv. 1–8), who retire afterwards with damsels to speak about love (v. 14). Cenne, in contrast, depicts clumsy nags (vv. 1–4), arrayed with meager décor by the peasants (vv. 5–8); and after the joust, the company must speak about farm animals (v. 14).

6. Sonetti de' Mesi: Di maggio

Il maggio voglio che facciate encagli[1]
con una gente di lavoratori,
con muli e gran destrier zoppecatori:[2]
per pettorali forti[3] reste di agli.
Intorno questo sianovi gran bagli
di villan scapigliati e gridatori,[4]
de'[5] qual[6] resolvan[7] sì fatti sudori,
che turbin[8] l'aere[9] sì che mai non cagli.
Poi altri villan,[10] facendovi[11] mance
di cipolle porraie[12] e di marroni,
usando in questo gran gavazze[13] e ciance:
en[14] giù letame ed[15] in alto forconi;
massari e veglie baciarsi le guance;
di pecore e di porci si ragioni.[16]

7. Sonetti de' Mesi: Di giugno

Di giugno siate in tale campagnetta
che ve[17] sien corbi ed[18] arghironcelli;[19]
le chiane intorno senza caravelli:
ed entro 'l mezzo[20] v'abbia[21] una isoletta,

---

[1] Navone: "en Cagli." Massèra and Vitale: "in Cagli."
[2] Massèra and Vitale: "zoppicatori."
[3] Neri: "forte."
[4] Navone: "cridatori."
[5] Navone and Neri: "dei."
[6] Massèra and Vitale: "quai."
[7] Massèra and Vitale: "risolvan."
[8] Navone and Neri: "turben."
[9] Neri: "l'aire."
[10] Navone: "vilan." Massèra and Vitale: "villan altri."
[11] Neri: "facendo."
[12] Navone, Neri, Massèra, and Vitale: "porrate."
[13] Navone and Neri: "cavazze."
[14] Massèra and Vitale: "e 'n."
[15] Neri: "et."
[16] Navone: "rasoni."
[17] Massèra: "vi."
[18] Navone and Neri: "et."
[19] Massèra and Vitale: "alghironcelli."
[20] Navone: "entro nel mezo." Neri: "entro 'l mezzo." Massèra and Vitale: "ed entro lo mezzo."
[21] Navone: "v'abia."

from which a small creek comes forth
that spreads out into a thousand streams
of sulfurous water, and such ponds
that it provides water to the entire area.[1]
And may bitter plums and shrubs be there,
raw medlar fruits and tasty dogwood berries—
may the streets all be muddy and narrow,
may the people all be black and gluttonous,
and may they behave rudely to each other
so that they're annoying to God and to the world.[2]

8. Sonnets of the Months: July

In July, I want you to be that crew
found in Orestano, with wines from the marshes,
with salt water and the strongest vinegars,
and fatty porks seasoned with peppers;
and then, after this, a vegetable salad
with sage and rosemary, to make you healthy,
fox meats poorly cooked in two sessions,
and, for whoever wanted it next, cabbage stew;

[1] Cenne structures the second stanza of this sonnet to evoke that of Folgore's June sonnet. He replaces Folgore's lovely mountain lake with one that smells of sulfur.

[2] The final two verses of the sonnet overturn the sentiment expressed by the last lines of Folgore's June sonnet. Instead of behaving with grace and courtesy, apparent to the whole world, they should act rudely and offend everyone.

de la qual esca sì forte vendetta,[1]
che 'n mille[2] parte[3] faccia ramicelli[4]
d'acqua di solfo, e cotai[5] gorgoncelli
sì ch'ella adacqui[6] ben tal contradetta.
E sorbi[7] e pruni acerbi siano lìe,
nespole crude e cornie savorose;
le rughe sian fangose e strette vie;
le genti ve[8] sian nere e gavinose,
e faccianvisi[9] tante villanie,
che a Dio ed al mondo siano noïose.[10]

8. Sonetti de' Mesi: Di luglio

Di luglio vo' che sia cotal brigata
en[11] Arestano, con vin di pantani,
con acque[12] salse ed[13] aceti soprani,
carne di porco grassa appeverata;[14]
e poi, diretro[15] a questo, una insalata
di salvi'[16] e ramerin per star più sani,
carne de[17] volpe guascotta a due mani
e a cui piacesse dietro,[18] cavolata;

1 Navone and Neri: "venetta."
2 Neri: "che mille."
3 Massèra and Vitale: "parti."
4 Navone and Neri: "e ramicelli."
5 Navone: "cotta in."
6 Navone: "adaqui."
7 Navone and Neri: "Sorbi."
8 Massèra and Vitale: "vi."
9 Navone and Neri: "faccianvesi."
10 Navone: "e al mondo siano noglose." Neri: "et al mondo siano nogliose."
11 Massèra and Vitale: "in."
12 Navone: "aque."
13 Navone and Neri: "et."
14 Massèra and Vitale: "a peverata."
15 Navone and Vitale: "di retro."
16 Navone and Neri: "salvie."
17 Massèra and Vitale: "di."
18 Navone: "drieto."

with long mantles in the style of hermits:
and may it be fiercely and terribly hot,
as when the sun is at the end of Leo.
And a hideous, avaricious lay monk
as chaperone who may be satisfied with such a life;
and may wives watch over everybody.[1]

9. Sonnets of the Months: August

In August I have you rest in the fresh air
of Sinigallia, which seems quite fine to me;
and in the day I give you, as medicine,
horseback riding for thirty miles,
all on bony trotters lacking saddles,
alongside foul-smelling water.
On the other hand, may you find bruises
when you return from this torment!
And if such repose doesn't stink to you,
I put you in Chiusi, sovereign city,
so tired that you can't unlace your clothes;

[1] As in Folgore's July sonnet, Cenne bestows many foods—but ill-prepared ones—on his company. In the last tercet of his sonnet, Folgore hopes his company would be free from watchful wives, while here Cenne imagines many wives watching over all his men.

con panni grossi lunghi de remita:[1]
e sia sì forte e sì terribil[2] caldo,
com'ha[3] il sol leone, a la fenita;
ed[4] un brutto converso per castaldo,
avaro, che si appaghi de[5] tal vita:
la moglie[6] a ciascadun sia 'n[7] manovaldo.

9. Sonetti de' Mesi: Di agosto

Di agosto vi reposo en[8] aere[9] bella,
en[10] Sinigallia,[11] che mi[12] par ben fina;
il giorno sì vi do, per medicina,
che cavalcate trenta migliatella,
e tutti en[13] trottier magri senza sella,
sempre lung'ad[14] un'acqua[15] de[16] sentina;
da l'altra parte, si faccia[17] tonnina,
poi ritornando a poso[18] di macella.
E se ben cotal poso[19] non vi annasa,
mettovi en[20] Chiusi, la città sovrana,
sì stanchi tutti da non disfar[21] l'asa;

---

1 Navone, Neri, Massèra, and Vitale: "d'eremita."
2 Massèra and Vitale: "terribile."
3 Navone and Neri: "com'à."
4 Navone and Neri: "et."
5 Massèra and Vitale: "di."
6 Navone: "mogle."
7 Navone: "in."
8 Massèra and Vitale: "riposo in."
9 Navone and Neri: "aire."
10 Massèra and Vitale: "in."
11 Navone and Neri: "Sinegallia."
12 Navone and Neri: "me."
13 Massèra and Vitale: "'n."
14 Neri: "lung'a."
15 Navone: "aqua."
16 Massèra: "un'acqua di." Vitale: "a un'acqua di."
17 Navone: "facci."
18 Navone: "pozzo." Neri: "puzzo."
19 Navone: "pozzo." Neri: "puzzo."
20 Massèra and Vitale: "in."
21 Navone: "diffare."

everyone's purse, tight and empty,
and to be like wolves with open mouths[1]
returning to Siena one day per week.

10. Sonnets of the Months: September

In September, I give you so many jewels,
needles and spindles, cumin[2] and belts;
night owls, falcons, and lame kites,
bows strung with wool, bent and heavy,
horned owls, barn owls and so many tawny owls,
as are to be found from here to Montpellier;
wool gloves and heavy purses—
always standing before your lady this way.
And to always buy and sell these things
frequenting merchants such as this;
to take such delights from September!
And to go through Siena yelling loudly:
"Whoever defends courtesy should die,
for the Salimbeni cast them out!"

11. Sonnets of the Months: October

In October I correctly suggest to you
that you reside in Falterona,
and that you eat the fruits there,
with its broad pans and quiet roosters.

[1] In the last tercet of Folgore's sonnet, he wishes that the company can enjoy the best foods because of their open-mouthed purses. Cenne, in contrast, wants them to be open-mouthed with hunger, like wolves, because of their empty purses.

[2] It is not clear why Cenne lists the spice cumin among the other objects in this sonnet. During the Middle Ages, there existed different beliefs about cumin that may be at play. Cumin was used medicinally as a plaster on the abdomen to treat digestive problems, and therefore Cenne may mention it to indicate again the company's bad foods. Conversely, cumin was viewed as effective in preventing chickens from escaping. Given the references to falconry throughout the poem, it may be that Cenne lists cumin here as a mistaken means to train falcons.

la borsa di ciascuno stretta e vana,
e stare come lupi a bocca pasa,
tornando en[1] Siena un dìe la semana.

10. Sonetti de' Mesi: Di settembre

Di settembre vi do gioielli alquanti:
àgor' e fusa, comino e asolieri;[2]
nottol' e[3] chieppe con nibbi lanieri;[4]
archi da lana bistorti e pesanti;
assiuoli,[5] barbagianni, allocchi[6] tanti,
quanti ne son de[7] qui a Monpeslieri:
guanti di lana, borse da braghieri:
stando così a vostra donna davanti.
E sempre questo comparar[8] e vendere,
con tali mercadanti il più usando:
e di settembre tal diletto prendere;
e per Siena entro gir alto gridando:[9]
—Mòia chi cortesia vuole[10] difendere,[11]
ch'i'[12] Salimbeni antichi li diêr bando!—

11. Sonetti de' Mesi: Di ottobre

Di ottobre vi conseglio[13] senza fallo
che ne la[14] Faltarona dimorate,
e de le frutta che vi son, mangiate
a teglie[15] grand'e[16] non vi canti[17] gallo.

---

1 Massèra and Vitale: "in."
2 Navone and Neri: "agore, fusa, cumino et aslieri."
3 Navone and Neri: "nottole."
4 Navone: "lamieri."
5 Navone: "asiuoli."
6 Navone and Neri: "alocchi."
7 Massèra and Vitale: "di."
8 Navone: "comparare."
9 Navone: "cridando."
10 Neri: "vole."
11 Navone and Neri: "defendere."
12 Navone: "che i."
13 Navone: "conseglo."
14 Navone: "nella."
15 Navone: "rigle." Neri, Massèra, and Vitale: "riglie."
16 Navone and Neri: "grande."
17 Navone and Neri: "canta."

The waters there are clear as crystal;
now drink, sons, and restore yourselves,
for there's good birdhunting there in the passes
that you'll toughen your necks in nerve and skin
in that air, which is clean and fine.
The Pisans are healthier in Pisa,
and the Genoese along the shore.
Don't be vain to my advice:
I'll give you a roast, mixed with ice[1]
so your hands and feet will feel the cold.

12. Sonnets of the Months: November

In November I put you in a large swamp[2]
where the cold Planet[3] has greatest influence,
with such poverty that you never will cease
struggling for money, which causes great harm.
May all your good foods be soggy there,
may your small candles be burned down to the green;[4]
chestnuts and sour apples from Faeta;
staying together with discord and complaining.

[1] The combination of a roast and ice is not entirely clear. Perhaps Cenne intends that there will be icy weather as the members of the company eat the roast.

[2] In place of Folgore's warm baths in November, Cenne places the company in a cold swamp.

[3] According to medieval astrology, the "cold Planet" was Saturn.

[4] Candles had a green line at the bottom, indicating when they needed to be replaced.

Chiare vi sono l'acque com'[1] cristallo:
or bevete, figliuoli, e ristorate;[2]
bono uccellar v'è[3] a' varchi, en[4] veritate,
ché farete[5] nel collo nervo e callo,
in quell'aere,[6] che[7] è sottile e fina:
ben stanno in[8] Pisa più chiari i pisani,
e 'l genovese lungo la marina.
Prendere 'l mi'[9] consej'[10] non siate[11] vani:
arrosto vi darò mesto con strina,
che 'l sentiranno i piedi con le mani.

12. Sonetti de' Mesi: Di novembre

Di novembre vi metto en[12] un gran stagno,
in qual parte più pò[13] fredda pianeta,
con quella povertà che non si acqueta[14]
di moneta acquistar, che fa gran dagno.[15]
Ogni buona vivanda ve sia in bagno;[16]
per lume, facelline[17] de[18] verdeta;
castagne con mele aspre di Faeta:
istando tutti ensieme en[19] briga e lagno.

---

1 Navone: "chiare l'aque vi son come." Neri, Massèra, and Vitale: "Chiare l'acque vi son come."

2 Navone and Neri: "restorate."

3 Navone: "uccellar bono è." Neri: "uccellar bono." Massèra and Vitale: "buon v'è uccellar."

4 Neri: "è 'n."

5 Neri: "fareti."

6 Navone and Neri: "aire."

7 Massèra and Vitale: "ched."

8 Neri: "en stanno en."

9 Navone: "prender el mio."

10 Navone: "consiglo." Neri and Massèra: "consiglio." Vitale: "consei'."

11 Massèra: "siá'."

12 Massèra and Vitale: "in."

13 Massèra and Vitale: "può."

14 Navone: "aqueta."

15 Navone, Neri, Massèra, and Vitale: "danno."

16 Navone, Neri, Massèra, and Vitale: "banno."

17 Navone: "faceline."

18 Massèra and Vitale: "di."

19 Massèra and Vitale: "in."

May there never be fires, but mud and chalk,[1]
and only in those places where the hermits are,
the nearest of which is twenty miles away;
and may you be lacking in bread and meat:
they avoid you as if you were the ugliest simpleton
seeing all of you living completely unfurnished.

13. Sonnets of the Months: December

In December I put you in a bog
with mud, ice, and few clothes,
beans and vetch as your consistent food—
as a tavern-keep, a Maremman pimp![2]
May an ugly, scrawny, sad and vain cook
give you undercooked neck meat—and little of it—
and may whoever among you pulls out dice or rooks
be considered a crafty man among sages.

[1] Cenne overturns this line in Folgore's November sonnet, in which he had given the company warm fires.

[2] In medieval Italy, the word "tavern-keep" was considered virtually synonymous with "pimp." See Rosella Omicciolo Valentini, *Mangiare nelle taverne medievali tra cibo, vino e giochi* (Tuscania: Edizioni penne e papiri, 2007): 10.

Fuoco non vi sia mai, ma fango e gesso,
se no 'n[1] alquanti luochi di rimiti,
che sia di venti miglia[2] lo più presso;
de[3] vin e[4] carne del tutto sforniti:
schernendo voi qual è più laido biesso,
veggendovi[5] star tutti sì sguarniti.

13. Sonetti de' Mesi: Di decembre

Di decembre[6] vi pongo en[7] un pantano
con fango, ghiaccia ed[8] ancor panni pochi;
per vostro cibo fermo, fave e mochi;
per oste abbiate[9] un troio maremmano.
Un cuoco brutto, secco,[10] tristo e vano,
ve[11] dia colli guascotti, e quelli,[12] pochi:
e qual tra voi allumi dadi o rochi
tenuto sia come tra savi un vano.

[1] Navone, Neri, Massèra, and Vitale: "non."
[2] Navone: "migla."
[3] Massèra and Vitale: "di."
[4] Navone: "di."
[5] Navone and Neri: "vegendovi."
[6] Massèra: "dicembre."
[7] Neri, Massèra, and Vitale: "in."
[8] Navone and Neri: "et."
[9] Navone: "abiate."
[10] Navone: "secho."
[11] Massèra: "che vi."
[12] Navone and Neri: "quigli." Massèra and Vitale: "quegli."

I give you tattered, filthy clothes;
among this group, everyone should wear on their heads
broken flasks, which fail at holding wine.
And everyone who sees you should marvel so
at seeing such dirty and unkempt people—
such young, beautiful men returning to Siena.

Panni rotti vi do e debrilati;[1]
appresso questo, ogni uomo[2] encappegli[3]
bottacci[4] a[5] vin da montanar fallati.
E chi ve[6] mira sì se[7] meravegli,[8]
vedendovi sì brutti rabbuffati,[9]
tornando in Siena così[10] bei fancegli.

1 Massèra and Vitale: "ed imbrillati."
2 Navone: "omo."
3 Navone: "en capegli." Massèra and Vitale: "incappegli."
4 Navone and Neri: "botti." Massèra and Vitale: "bottazzi."
5 Navone and Neri: "de."
6 Massèra and Vitale: "vi."
7 Massèra and Vitale: "si."
8 Navone: "meravigli."
9 Neri: "rabuffati."
10 Navone: "cusì."

Chapter Three: Pietro dei Faitinelli, Nicknamed Il Mugnone[1] (ca. 1285–90 / 1349)

[1] Cited from Mario Marti's *Poeti giocosi del tempo di Dante*, with the variants from Massèra and Vitale in the notes. Two other editors, Leone del Prete and Anna Paola Zilli, reproduce two versions each of Pietro's sonnets, representing the Tuscan and Venetian manuscript traditions; to have included their dialect variants in the notes, however, would have proven unwieldy. See Leone del Prete, ed., *Rime di Ser Pietro de' Faytinelli detto Mugnone, poeta lucchese del sec. XIV* (Bologna: Romagnoli, 1874); and Anna Paola Zilli, ed., "Pietro de' Faitinelli, *Le Rime*," *Quaderni lucchesi di studi sul medioevo e sul rinascimento* 1:1 (gennaio-giugno 2000): 11–104.

Canzone **#1:** A critique of contemporary life, which has lost the traditional values of medieval nobility (courtesy, *largesse*, gentleness). Instead, market success has replaced Christian virtues, to the extent that the legendary thieves Giriello and Salvagno would now be viewed positively.

1.

Courtesy is dead, *largesse* is dead,
gentleness is dead,
honor is dead, as are many fine customs,
which used to be found in finer times.
Truth is banished and loyalty disdained,
piety is defeated by impiety
and our hearts are blinded in their eyes,
and that's how things move backwards.
The evilest betrayals and tricks,
which used to be done for greed,
are now considered a greater wisdom.
If Giriello and Salvagno lived today,
their loot would be considered clean earnings.

Rich fools are considered wise sages—
that's what we've come to—
and those who are adorned with knowledge
are avoided whenever they lack wealth.
Great deeds have entirely disappeared,
and middle and low ones
are tossed aside without recognition,
which dries up the source of piety.
Blood relations no longer have any place,
nor brotherhood, nor love of party.
I have filled a thousand papers with this,
and I shout from the rooftops;
everyone says, "Go on, it'll turn out fine."

Love of neighbor and of God
disappeared a long time ago,
without which whoever wants to rise

1.

Spent'è la cortesia, spent'è larghezza,[1]
spent'è la gentilezza,
spent'è l'onore e[2] molti be' costumi,
ch'usar[3] al tempo buon già si soleano.
Lo vero è 'n bando e lealtà si sprezza,
vint'è pietà da empiezza,
sì son de' nostri cori orbati i lumi,
e sì per ritrosie le cose vanno.
Lo tradimento pessimo e lo 'nganno,
che farsi[4] suol per ghiottornia d'avere,
tenuto è più sapere;
e se vivesse Girello e Salvagno
terrìensi[5] i furti lor netto guadagno.

Li ricchi stolti son savi tenuti,
a tanto siàn venuti;
e que' che sono ornati di scïenza,
sono schifati abbiendo povertate.
Gli gran servigi tutti son perduti,
e' mezzani e minuti
son postergati per disconoscenza,
che fa seccar la fonte di pietate.
Non ci ha più loco consanginitate,
non fratellanza, né amor di parte.
Di questo ho mille carte,
e simigliante dico delle tette.
Ognun dice: "Va, va, che ben gli mette."

La carità del prossimo e di Dio
molt'è che dispario,
senza la quale indarno s'affatica

---

[1] Massèra's edition does not contain this *canzone*.
[2] Vitale: "e'."
[3] Vitale: "ch'usare."
[4] Vitale: "far si."
[5] Vitale: "teriensi."

to the eternal realm struggles in vain.
I can't forget about lust and pomp,
nor the evil sin
of avarice, God's mortal enemy,
wherever it whets our intellect.
Today, virtues are viewed with disdain,
and vices and the wicked
are both commended.
Why do I go on with so many words?
God, nor saints, nor holy women are feared.

Therefore, if evil rides on the back of goodness,
which undoubtedly is taking place,
what person on earth would be amazed
if the earth doesn't produce its fruits?
The marvel is that God still allows
our filth and intrigues,
and how can He mitigate His anger
that He doesn't send the whole world to the depths?
Where else is Christianity being led
if not to schism, tyranny, theft, and war,
and from that we are not freed:
and if no remedy comes from God, I see
that the world will go from bad to worse.

Now go, my new moral *canzonetta*,
which is easy to understand,
to those places where good men are,
the holy, and wise with knowledge;
and if you're about to be read by others,
throw yourself out of their hands
so that your valor isn't heard in their ears.
You would throw your words to the wind,
since the mad never want correction,
and the wise always do the opposite
and keep it in their armory.
You will be understood by the wise,
and defended with reason, and not with swords.

chi vuol salire nello eterno regno.
Lascivie e pompe non metto in oblio
né quel peccato rio
d'avaricia, di Dio[1] mortal nemica,
ove s'aguza[2] tutto il nostro ingegno.
Virtù ci son tenute quasi a sdegno;
e vizii e viziosi scelerati,
costor son commendati.
Perché me infrasco[3] di parole tante?
temuto non c'è Iddio, santi né sante.

Dunque se il male ci cavalca il bene,
che senza dubbio avvène,
qual uom terren dovria maravigliarsi,
se la terra non rende lo suo frutto?
La maraviglia è pur che Dio sostiene
nostre spurcizie e mene,
e come l'ira sua può mitigarsi,
ch'e' non profonda giù il secol tutto.
Ov'è ad altro il cristianesmo addutto
ch'a scisma, tirannia, rapina e guerra?
E da ciò non si sferra:
E se da Dio non n'è riparo, veggio
che il mondo è per andar di male in peggio.

Vanne, moral mia nova canzonetta,
da intender leggeretta,
in quelle parti dove siano i buoni
di santi e savi con conoscimento.
E se dagli altri tu vuogl'esser letta,
fuor di lor man ti getta,
che in lor orecchi tuo valor non suoni.
Ché tu gittresti le parole al vento,
ché il matto non vuol mai correggimento,
e 'l saggio[4] sempre fa tutto el contrario,
e tiello nel suo armario.
Da' buon sarai con diligenza intesa,
e senza spade con ragion difesa.

---

[1] Vitale: "d'avarizia, d'Iddio."
[2] Vitale: "s'aguzza."
[3] Vitale: "mi 'nfrasco."
[4] Vitale: "savio."

Sonnets #2–4: The traditional motif of misogyny.

2.

A man can know physics and nature well,
the law with its decrees and decretals,
and get a doctorate in Divine Scripture,
or in all of the seven liberal arts,
necromancy, alchemy, or augury,
the properties of birds or of animals,
and the virtues of herbs and what they can cure,
and the value of oriental gemstones.
Woman, however, in my opinion—
I don't know who understands her fully,
so dark and faithless are her words.
Because all of the knowledgeable prophets
and all of the men there are under the sun,
they were all evilly tricked by women.

3.

In good truth, it isn't at all clear to me—
even though Holy Scripture allows it—
that women might even see paradise,
nor even come close enough to heat things up inside,
nor that God the Father made their faces
in the image of His holy figure;
instead, through a specific sacrament,
was woman a diabolic creation.
Woman is the root of all entrapment,
woman is the one who adores all fraud;
women dream up all evil and do it.

2.

Om[1] può saper ben fisica e natura
e legge con Decreto e Decretali,
e conventare en[2] divina Scrittura
e in tutte sette l'arti liberali,
nigromanzia, alchìmia o ver d'augura,
e propietà d'uccelli o di animali,
e le vertù de l'erb' e che[3] 'l procura,
e 'l pregio de le gemme orientali.
Ma femmena,[4] secondo mia parvenza,
non saccio chi conosca enteramente,
tanto ha fallaci e grige sue parole:
ché de' profeta pieni di sapienza
e d'uomini[5] quant'e' n'ha sotto al sole,
gabbati ne remanser malamente.

3.

En bona[6] verità, non m'è avviso,
avvegna ch'ello piaccia a la Scrittura,
che femmena[7] pur veggia il paradiso,
che non v'appressi a far dentro calura;
né che Deo padre li formasse 'l viso
a simiglianza de la sua figura:
anzi fu, per sacramento preciso,
femmena[8] dïabolica fattura.
La femmen'è[9] radice de l'enganno;[10]
femmen'è[11] quella che ogni fraude affetta;
femmene[12] pensan ogni mal e fanno.

---

[1] Vitale: "Uom."
[2] Massèra and Vitale: "in."
[3] Massèra and Vitale: "l'erbe, chi."
[4] Massèra and Vitale: "femmina."
[5] Massèra and Vitale: "ed uomini."
[6] Massèra and Vitale: "In buona."
[7] Massèra and Vitale: "femmina."
[8] Massèra and Vitale: "la femmina."
[9] Massèra and Vitale: "femmin'è."
[10] Massèra and Vitale: "inganno."
[11] Massèra and Vitale: "femmin'è."
[12] Massèra and Vitale: "femmine."

But still I have this firm and clear belief
that some— but they are few— go there
to not leave Holy Mary there all by herself.

4.

I don't deny, Death— you, who are common to all—
that you do not have *largesse* and courtesy,
for you entered into my lady's body;
and if I were ungrateful, I would be wrong!
But she was a friend so special to you
and always kept faith with you
that you shouldn't have broken faith with her.
Now— deny that you are disloyal!
Tell me how, and where, your entry was,
and your exit, because she had more difficult passes—
tighter too— than those between Cordova and Grenada.[1]
It is a great marvel to me that you entered
and that you didn't drown in there:
I believe, Death, that you despaired inside her.

Sonnet #5: Basing himself on Folgore's sonnet, "I don't praise you, God, and I don't adore you" (#29), Pietro withholds his adoration due to the corrupt state of society. In it he echoes the medieval Christian belief that the Prophet Mohammed's body was suspended in the air in Mecca by means of magnetism.

5.

Hercules, Apollo, Vesta, and Minerva
I want to adore, and renounce the faith
of that wrongful God, in Whom all believe,
for He's not right, nor does He follow reason.

[1] That is to say, the Strait of Gibraltar.

Ma ben i' ho[1] credenza ferma e netta
che alquante, ma ben poche, ve ne vanno,
per non lassar santa Maria soletta.

4.

Eo[2] non sconfesso, Morte comunale,
che pur tegna[3] dono e cortesia,
ch'entrasti en[4] corpo de la donna mia;
e s'eo[5] ne fosse ingrato, farei male.
Ma era sì tua amica speciale
e stata sempre a la speranza tia,
che non li dovei romper compagnia:
or disdì poi che non se' misliale!
Deh dimme[6] come ed onde fo[7] tua entrata
e gita, ché v'avia più forti passi
e stretti, che tra Còrduba e Granata.
Gran meraviglia parmi che v'entrassi,
e più che non vi se' dentro affogata:
ben credo, Morte, che ti desperassi!

5.

Ercol, Timbrëo,[8] Vesta e la Minerva
voglio adorare e renegar[9] la fede
di quel tortoso Deo, nel qual uom crede,
che non è dritto, né ragion osserva.

---

1 Massèra and Vitale: "ben ho."
2 Massèra and Vitale: "Io."
3 Massèra and Vitale: "pur non tegna."
4 Massèra and Vitale: "'n."
5 Massèra and Vitale: "s'io."
6 Massèra and Vitale: "dimmi."
7 Massèra and Vitale: "fu."
8 Massèra: "Cibele."
9 Massèra and Vitale: "rinnegar."

I want to become a Jew and a servant
of the sect of Arius or Fotino his follower,
the tyrant Nero, Herod, and Diomedes,
and stingy Medea, the pitiless.
I intend to end my life in Mecca,
there where Mohammed lies and is suspended
in the air by the virtue of a magnet;
for I see the evil raised up and the good laid low,
righteousness, faith and loyalty be killed,
and men offended by their servants.

6.

Just because a man has a nice face, or laughs,
or joyfully gives you a greeting,
don't proclaim him to be a friend right away,
and if you're at war, don't let him lead you.
Because words are merely wind, and shouts,
when they are pronounced, cost nothing;
thus it should cost the value of a tooth
to them, and to whomever trusts in them.
Because the whole world is filled with treason,
with false appearances, and with pretense—
enough to dry hats with its nice wind.
And this is the sense of my sentences:
whoever trusts on sight or on appearances,
without any other proof, makes a thousand errors.

Sonnets #7–15: About the warfare between the Guelph city of Lucca and the Ghibelline city of Pisa. In his poems, Pietro derides the weakness of the Guelph league and their leader, King Roberto II of Naples (King Berta), the son of Charles I who lost control of Sicily in the uprising of 1266 known as the Sicilian Vespers. He criticizes the Guelphs, divided into the White and Black factions, and decries the betrayal of Lucca by the Pogginghi and Quartigiani families. He portrays the invasion of Lucca, where Gherardo da San Lupidio ("the Vicar") dropped the Guelph standard and fled, followed by Pier d'Eboli. He reminds the Guelphs of the famous victims of traitors, such as Count Ugolino della Gherardesca of Pisa, betrayed by the Archbishop Ruggieri (an event famously recalled by Dante in *Inferno* 32–33), and the Milanese Lords of the Tower (Torrioni), who were ousted by the Visconti in the thirteenth century. Pietro also worries about the ascendancy of the Pisan forces under Uguccione dalla Faggiuola and his general, Castruccio Castracani, and sees them as avenging the deaths of the Emperor Frederick II's heirs, Conrad and Manfred, at the hands of the Guelphs.

Giudeo vo' deventare[1] e di conserva
di setta d'Ario[2] e di Fotino erede,
Nerone[3] tiranno, Erode e Dïomede
e senza pïetà Medea proterva.
A Mecca intendo di finir mia vita,
là o' Macometto giace e sta sospeso
en aere per vertù[4] de calamita.
Ch'i' veggio 'l reo montato e 'l bon[5] desceso;
drittura, fé, leanza esser perita;
e da cui l'uomo serve essere offeso.

6.

Per ch'om[6] ti mostri bel piacer o rida
e dóneti[7] saluto allegramente,
non l'appellar amico mantenente,
e s' tu sei 'n guerra, nol ti far tua guida.
Ché le parole son vento e le grida,
e 'n su quel punto non costan nïente;
così costasse la profferta un dente
a quei cotali e chi di lor se[8] fida!
Ché tutto 'l mondo è pien di tradimento
con false viste e con infingardie,
e d'asciugar berrette ad un bel vento.
E quest'è 'l sòn[9] de le sentenzie mie:
chiunque se fida en[10] vista o mostramento
senz'altra prova, fa mille follie.

---

1 Massèra and Vitale: "diventare."
2 Massèra: "d'arianiste." Vitale: "arïaniste."
3 Massèra and Vitale: "Neron."
4 Massèra and Vitale: "in aere per virtù."
5 Massèra and Vitale: "buon."
6 Massèra and Vitale: "uom."
7 Massèra and Vitale: "dòniti."
8 Massèra and Vitale: "si."
9 Massèra and Vitale: "quest'è suon."
10 Massèra and Vitale: "chiunqua si fida in."

Under the Imperial standard of the Eagle, which has just been victorious in San Salvi, he foresees the victory of the Ghibellines throughout Italy.

7.

Egotism and pride reign a short time
because Christ will put an end to them;
and we have a true symbol of this—
Lucifer was cast down from on high.
Charles, through his excesses and haughtiness
lost Sicily, which was his dominion;
in Pisa every mind should still remember
that noble Count Ugolino was killed.
And here's another example of it:
those of the Tower, Lords of Milan,
were destroyed by their great arrogance.
So I counsel those who are on top
to have humility and temperance,
and not to oppress their peers or subjects.

8.

The lazy king, Charles's heir— but not of his valor—
should not hope, if the Guelphs' status changes,
to keep his realm, Apulia, and the Principality,
Abruzzo nor Calabria, as he thinks.
Nor should he try to set foot in Provence;
both the east and the west will be taken from him.
Conrad and King Manfred will be paid back
by the Blacks and Ghibellines without mercy.
He should stay in Naples or Aversa,
in Capua, Teano, or in Calvi if he likes,
because the Eagle has just shaken San Salvi.

7.

L'orgoglio e la soperbia[1] poco regna,
che Cristo non gli ponga suo termìno;
di ciò potem veder verace ensegna:[2]
Lucifero ne fu messo al declino.
Carlo, per suo oltraggio o gran desdegna,[3]
perdeo Cicilia, ch'era in suo domino;
ancor en[4] Pisa, mentre ciascun tegna,
morto ne fu 'l gentil conte Ugolino.
Eccon'un altro esempio a[5] simiglanza:
quei da la Torre, de Melan[6] segnori,
destrutti fôr[7] per lor tropp'arroganza.
Però conseglio quei che son maggiori,
che abbian umiltà[8] e temperanza,
non soperchiando lor par né minori.

8.

Non speri 'l pigro re di Carlo erede,
non del valor, se 'l guelfo muta stato,
tener lo regno, Puglia e 'l Principato,
Abruzzo, né Calabria, come crede.
Né in Provenza pensi metter piede;
levante con ponente i fie levato;
Currado e 'l re Manfred' i fie mertato
da' neri e ghibellin senza merzede.
Stïasi pur en Napoli o en[9] Aversa,
en[10] Capüa, Teano o vòl in Calvi:
ché l'aquila ha ghermito già San Salvi.

---

[1] Massèra and Vitale: "superbia."
[2] Massèra and Vitale: "insegna."
[3] Massèra and Vitale: "disdegna."
[4] Massèra and Vitale: "in."
[5] Massèra and Vitale: "e."
[6] Massèra and Vitale: "di Milan."
[7] Massèra: "distrutti fûr." Vitale: "distrutti fur."
[8] Massèra and Vitale: "umiltade."
[9] Massèra and Vitale: "in Napoli o in."
[10] Massèra and Vitale: "in."

Alas, it makes me feel faint just to say it—
the Guelph party was dispersed,
now let him preach, and recite primes and terces.

9.

If we go to battle, my heart has faith
that we'll win, because we are in the right;
we have three of the king's sons as our leaders,
and a million men, brave like the paladins,
who won't turn tail from the German war cries
that at another time frightened us.
Whoever captures Uguccione, don't kill him,
but lead him to prison in Florence;
and the same thing should be done with the Guelphs,
Pisans and Lucchese, who betrayed their lands:
the cursed Pogginghi and Quartigiani.
May their conflict be unleashed in all of Italy!
And send home others without eyes or hands
in eternal memory of this war.

10.

Since you're broken on the crags by the shore,
Guelphs, because of your foolish navigation,
don't dismay of that bad alliance:
struggle to round up another pack
of that Frankish people, which doesn't avoid
the sight of the Germans who make you tremble;
but this should be written in your hearts always:
you should never disdain your enemies.
Now hear this terrible punishment:
whoever can't see how it goes needs to flee;
hear, for even the doctrine is correct.

Oimè, ché sol a dirlo par ch'i' smalvi!
La parte guelfa fu en esser dispersa:
or sermoneggi e dica prima e tersa.

9.

Se si combatte, el meo core se[1] fida
de[2] vincer, per ch'avèm piena ragione,
e tre figliuoi di re per nostra guida
e gente paladina un milïone,
da non fuggir per le tedesche strida,
le qual[3] ci spaventâr una stagione;
chi Uguccion prenderà, pur non l'uccida,
ma menilo in Fierenze[4] per pregione.
e simil faccia de' guelfi pisani
e de' lucchesi, ca tradîr lor terra,
Pogginghi maladetti e Quartigiani.
Per tutta Italia lor briga si sferra!
E gli altri mandi senza occhi né mani,
ad eterna memoria d'esta guerra.

10.

Poi rotti sète a scoglio presso a riva,
guelfi, per vostro sciocco navigare,
non sbigottite di setta cattiva:
brigate un altro stuolo di raunare
di quella franca gente, che non schiva
todesca[5] vista, che vi fa tremare;
ma questo en[6] vostro cor sempre si scriva,
che non si dé' nemico desdegnare.[7]
Di che sentite grossa disciplina:
chi non guata com' va, convèn si fugga;
udite, ch'anco è bòna[8] la dottrina.

[1] Massèra and Vitale: "il mio core si."
[2] Massèra and Vitale: "di."
[3] Massèra and Vitale: "quai."
[4] Massèra and Vitale: "Firenze."
[5] Massèra and Vitale: "tedesca."
[6] Massèra and Vitale: "in."
[7] Massèra and Vitale: "disdegnare."
[8] Massèra and Vitale: "buona."

Lord, do you want to see destroyed
the traitorous maritime Hare?
Here, other arms are needed rather than flight.

11.

I seem to already see Faggiuola
king of Tuscany: I mean Uguccione,
who could school all the foxes in cunning.
And I seem to hear all the people yell:
"Death to the Guelphs, out, out! You scoundrel!
Death to King Berta, that stingy merchant!"
I see the Vicar throw down the standard,
and Messer Pier fleeing without the flag.
And I see burnings, stabbings, robbing and privation
of men and women and children in their cribs,
and the name of Guelph silenced throughout Italy.
Berta sells us to fill up Bruna[1]
even more; but for one thing I'm happy:
Frederick will take everything that he collects!

12.

Wars were never won by making threats,
nor by closing purses, in my opinion,
nor by sleeping, nor by going about adorned,
staring at the young maidens of Florence;
nor by shouting, "Long live the Prince!,"
nor by gambling, nor remaining divided;
but by uniting and by showing one's face—
through wisdom, through *largesse*, and forethought.
If you follow my advice, you'll be on top
of the Hare that makes you scratch your temples
if it doesn't diminish your options first.

[1] Bruna: The tower in which the royal treasure was kept.

Signor, volete voi che si destrugga
la traditrice lèpore marina?
Qui fa mestèr[1] altre arme, che di fugga.

11.

Veder mi par già quel da la Faggiuola
re di Toscana: eo[2] dico d'Uguccione,
il qual terria le volpe tutte a scòla;[3]
e parme[4] udir gridar già le persone:
— Muoiano i guelfi! fòr fòr,[5] mariuola!
muoia re Berta, quell'avar treccone! —
Veggio 'l vicar gittar giù la mazzuola,
e misser Pier fuggir senza 'l pennone.
E veggio incendio, taglia, ruba e stento
d'uomini e donne e fanciulli di cuna,
e 'n tutta Italia el[6] guelfo nome spento.
Berta ci vende per empir la Bruna
ben meglio; ma per un ne sto contento:
che Federico avrà ciò ch'e' rauna.

12.

Già per minacce guerra non vénze[7]
né per la borsa stringer, ciò m'è avviso,
né per dormir, né per andar assiso
mirando le donzelle per Fierenze;[8]
non per gridar: — Viva viva el prenze! —
non per giucar, né per istar doviso:
ma per unirsi e per mostrar lo viso,
per senni, per larghezze e provvidenze.
Di sopra siete, se 'l mio dir s'adempie,
in quanto non vi attuti lo dispendio
la lepre, che vi fa grattar le tempie.

---

[1] Massèra and Vitale: "mestier."
[2] Massèra and Vitale: "io."
[3] Massèra and Vitale: "scuola."
[4] Massèra and Vitale: "parmi."
[5] Massèra and Vitale: "fuor fuor."
[6] Massèra and Vitale: "il."
[7] Massèra and Vitale: "non si vénze."
[8] Massèra and Vitale: "Firenze."

I've condensed much in this small space:
God purified you of your impious acts the other day
with eternal death and fire from Pisa.

Sonnet #13: A critique of the Florentine Guelphs: Pietro accuses them of being more interested in commerce— displaying vain ostentation, manufacturing woolen goods, accumulating florins, and living a sumptuous life— than of defeating the Ghibellines.

13.

You go about most bravely on display
with helmets and crests plated in silver,
and you seem to want to take the lion
in the middle of Florence when you joust.
In order to glorify your homeland—
and there's no other today so honored—
you hide away in your holes like rabbits,
and you hide your faces when you should show them.
Leave warfare to the Perugians,
and you should always amuse yourself with wool
and with pleasures and with collecting florins.
You used to subjugate all of Tuscany;
now you are not worth three coins in weapons,
if not about striking the quintain.[1]

14.

Although I'm not a castrato, Castruccio
castrated me when Lucca was betrayed,
so all lustfulness exited from my loins,
and, for that reason, I live now chastely.
I figure the accounts with three beans,
but without multiplying on my fingers;

[1] The quintain was a practice target for jousting. However, the expression "to strike the quintain" was used as a euphemism for sexual intercourse. Pietro seems to use the expression with such a meaning in this sonnet, indicating the decadence of the Florentine Guelphs.

Eo ho[1] compreso assai 'n breve compendio:
Dio vi purgò l'altrier de l'opre émpie
per eternal di Pisa morte e encendio.[2]

13.

Voi gite molto arditi a far la mostra
con elmi e con cimiere inargentate,
e par che lo leon prender vogliate
per Firenze entro, quando fate giostra.
E per magnificar la terra vostra,
che non n'è oggi de le più onorate,
a guisa di conigli vi entanate,[3]
e 'l viso, ove si dée, non si demostra.[4]
Lassate far la guerra a' perugini,
e voi v'entramettete[5] de la lana
e de[6] goder e raunar fiorini.
Voi solevate soggiogar Toscana;
or non valete en[7] arme tre fiorini,
se non a ben ferir per la quintana.

14.

Sì mi castrò, per ch'io non sia castrone,
Castruccio, quando Lucca fu tradita,
che de' mei[8] lombi è la lussuria uscita,
e vivo en[9] castità per sua cagione.
Con tre lupin del mio faccio ragione,
e senza alcun multiplicar di dita;

[1] Massèra and Vitale: "I'ho."
[2] Massèra and Vitale: "incendio."
[3] Massèra and Vitale: "v'intanate."
[4] Massèra and Vitale: "dimostra."
[5] Massèra and Vitale: "v'intramettete."
[6] Massèra and Vitale: "di."
[7] Massèra and Vitale: "in."
[8] Massèra and Vitale: "miei."
[9] Massèra and Vitale: "in."

tax collectors no longer call on me,
nor do pikesmen pester me for tolls.
I thank and praise him for all of this;
but he submitted his city to Pisa
and to a tyrant more cruel than Herod.
And it found no humanity there
though he could have passed through another way;
for this he should accept what thanks come his way.

15.

Wherever should I find games and pleasures?
Wherever should I find talk with laughter?
Where, if not torments of all types?
Where should I find what doesn't craze me?
Will I ever have news that pleases me?
No, from what my heart can foresee.
For I see my Lucca made an outpost of Pisa,
and lords turned into the servants of pageboys.
I see it defiled, nude and inhabited
not by its ancient inhabitants,
but by those who've so misguided it.
And I can't seem to see even a leaf or flower,
due to my desire to return there so quickly:
and I feel great envy of those who die there.

Sonnet #16: The yearning to return to Lucca from exile.

16.

If I see my return to fair Lucca,
which will be when the fresh pear is rotten,
no such happiness in a human heart
has there ever been as much as I'll have then.
I'll go about kissing the city walls,
and men too, weeping for happiness:

messo di gabellier più non mi cita,
né per lo dazio temo di piccone.
Di ciò c'ho detto, lui rengrazio[1] e lodo;
ma sottomise a Pisa sua cittade,
ed al crudel tiranno più che Rodo.[2]
E non vi fu trovato umanitade,
potendosi passar per altro modo:
di questo abbia quel grato che vi cade!

15.

Onde mi dée venir giuochi e sollazzi?
onde mi dée venir motti con risa?
onde, se non tormenti d'ogni guisa?
onde mi dée venir, se non ch'eo[3] impazzi?
Avròe mai novella che mi agazzi?
No, secondo che lo meo core avvisa:[4]
ché veggio Lucca mia castel di Pisa,
e' signor fatti servi de' ragazzi.
Veggiola ontata, nuda ed abitata
non da lo suo antico abitatore,
ma da color che l'hanno sì guidata.
E non mi par veder fronde né fiore
di far così per fretta la tornata:
ond'io porto asto grande a chi ci mòre.[5]

16.

S'eo veggio en[6] Lucca bella mio ritorno,
che fi' quando la pera fie ben mézza,
en nullo còre[7] uman tant'allegrezza
già mai non fu, quant'eo[8] avrò quel giorno.
Le mura andrò leccando d'ogn'intorno
e gli uomini, piangendo d'allegrezza;

[1] Massèra and Vitale: "ringrazio."
[2] Massèra and Vitale: "ch'Erodo."
[3] Massèra and Vitale: "ch'io."
[4] Massèra: "che 'l mio cuore s'avvisa." Vitale: "che 'l meo core s'avvisa."
[5] Massèra and Vitale: "muore."
[6] Massèra and Vitale: "S'io veggio in."
[7] Massèra and Vitale: "in nullo cuore."
[8] Massèra and Vitale: "io."

hate, rancor, strife and all impiety
I will set aside against those who banished me.
And I will prefer coarse bread there
to the finest loaves found anywhere else;
instead of featherbeds elsewhere, there a bedframe.
Because I've eaten such a bitter morsel,
and I will feel it as long as I'm exiled,
that my brothers are the Ghibellines and the Whites.

Frottola #17: A social satire about the changes that have occurred in Lucca since coming under the control of Castruccio Castracani. The identities of most of these individuals have not been determined.

17.

I can't say that I don't live troubled
for I was born in Lucca,
but my hand is kept away from the gaming table
when my heart remembers
what wisdom and valor
and noble blood have become;

and Truglio and Puglio and Mastin Farinato,
Faben, Britto and Casato,
Migliaio and Argomento were lords,
and Maestrello the weaver, Puccin the dyer
and Cuper the cartman,
Nuta, Feccia, Antel, Vestito and Dato,

Gigliotto the blacksmith, Ner, Chele Accordato,
Cinel, Din, Bigi, and Mato,
Cin the sweeper and Vita the porter;
listen, famous city, for the love I bear you,
so I may reacquire my honor:
Lucca, it's more pleasant there than in the other state.
Now, no gangs, no thefts can be committed
by Vippa, Ser Lippo, Lotto, Ser Comuccio,
Guercio, Michel, Borguccio,
Bontur, nor Pecchio who cleaned the streets.

odio, rancore, guerra ed ogni empiezza
porrò giù contra quei che mi cacciorno.
    E qui me' voglio 'l bretto castagniccio,
'nanzi ch'altrove pan di gran calvello;
'nanzi ch'altrove piume, qui il graticcio.
    Ch'i' ho provato sì amaro morsello,
e provo e proverò, stando esiticcio,
che 'l bianco e 'l ghibellin vo' per fratello.

17.

    Io non vo' dir ch'i' non viva turbato,
ch'io son di Lucca nato
e tengo del taulier la man di fore:
ma quando mi rimetto ben per core
come 'l senno e 'l valore
e 'l nobil sangue v'era diventato;

e Tuglio[1] e Puglio e Mastin, Farinato,
Faben, Britto e Casato,
Migliaio e Argomento eran signore,
e 'l Maestrello cestai', Puccin tintore
e Cuper carratore,[2]
Nuto, il Feccia, Antel, Vestito e Dato,

Gigliotto fabbro, Ner, Chele, Accordato,
Cinel, Din, Bigi, e Mato,
Cin pattumaio e Vita portatore;
odi, città gridata, per mio amore:
s'i' riacquisti mio onore,
Lucca, è più da piacer che 'n l'altro stato.
    Or non vi può far leghe e furerie
Vippa, ser Lippo, Lotto e ser Comuccio,
Guercio, Michel, Borguccio,
Bontur né Pecchio, che spazzò le vie;

---

[1] Massèra and Vitale: "Truglio."
[2] Massèra and Vitale: "carradore."

Nor can Nello, the low-born merchant
blossom through strength of the companies,
nor can he stay there
and suck in goods like an open-mouthed fish.

Now, may noble Castruccio have a good hour and year
for it was he
to put down this strife;
he's put out all these small tyrannies.

***Tenzone* with L. of Pisa (sonnets #18A-B):** Pietro makes a political prediction by allegorizing the cities of Tuscany: the Lion represents Florence; the Horse is Arezzo; the She-bear is Pistoia; the Panther represents Lucca; the Mastiff indicates the lord of Verona Mastino I of the Scala family; the Hare is Pisa; and the She-wolf is Siena. The identity of the poet L. of Pisa is not known.

18A. To L. of Pisa

The Lion goes roaring through the forest:
he has his head lifted for joy,
and has the free-reined Horse beneath him;
he plays and rejoices with the She-bear.
And the Panther lends him its valor,
and has given him some from the side
because the Mastiff has commanded it;
and this is now known to everyone.
The Hare needs to keep a watchful eye,
for the Lion and the She-wolf now hate her;
they've cast their nets and want to catch her.
And they have firm agreements about this:
this time it will do her no good to flee
as she knows how to do, nor to play one against the other.
The Lion and the She-wolf are in position
to consume the Hare and destroy her.

né Nello, marcenai'[1] popolaruccio,
germoglia per vigor di compagnie,
né pòte star colìe
per tôrre a bocca aperta come 'l luccio.

Deh che ben abbia l'anno, l'ora e 'l dìe,
che fu signore il nobile Castruccio,
a poner giù il cruccio:
c'ha tutte spente queste tirannie.

18A. A L. da Pisa

Mugghiando va il leon per la foresta:
per allegressa egli ha 'l capo levato,
ed ha sotto[2] 'l caval ch'è disfrenato;
con l'orsa si trastulla e fa gran festa.
E la pantera del valor li presta
e parte ne li ha dato da l'un lato,
per che 'l mastin di ciò l'ha comandato:
e questo pure è cosa manifesta.
Conviensi omai la lepre di guardare;
il leone e la lupa odi c'han fatto:
tes'ha[3] le reti e vòglionla pigliare.
E di questo son fermi ad ogni patto;
non li varrà 'l fuggir ch'ella sa fare,
né 'l giucar de le volte, questo tratto.
Il leone e la lupa in posta stanno
per consumar la lepre e farli danno.

---

[1] Massèra and Vitale: "marcenaio."
[2] Massèra and Vitale: "seco."
[3] Massèra and Vitale: "tes'han."

18B. From L. of Pisa

Friend, make sure that it isn't a headache
or that it isn't some sort of pain
that is making Lion roar, or another ill fate
that perhaps causes him such great trouble.
To make so much noise for happiness,
as you say, because the Panther
gave him its own things not out of pleasure
but to show how obedient it is,
wouldn't be smart; because if he wants
to count clearly, he will find out how
negotiations cause more pain than pleasure.
The one who spurs him quickly should take care
not to ride the Horse without a rein madly,
as he usually does, often bareback.
The Hare is happy, nor does she fear traps
of nets that the false ones have spread out.
The sharp Hare with its wisdom and prudence
fears not She-wolf nor Lion nor She-bear.

18B. L. da Pisa

Amico, guarda non sia mal di testa
o che nol punga suo dolor usato,
per che a mugghiar si mova, o altro fato,
che forse 'l[1] tuo leon forte molesta.
Ché menar d'allegressa tal tempesta,
come tu di', per che gli abbia donato
la pantera del suo, non per suo grato,
ma per mostrarsi ne l'ubbidir presta,
non seria senno: ché, se annoverare
chiaro vuol', vedera' che del baratto
doler si può vie più che rallegrare.
Guardisi non cavalchi come matto,
senza freno, il cavallo, come[2] suol fare
talor di schiena, a chi lo sprona ratto.
La lepre allegra sta, né teme inganno
di reti, che quei falsi tese li hanno.
L'arguta lepre, con suo senno e forsa,
non teme lupa né 'l leon né l'orsa.

[1] Massèra and Vitale: "il."
[2] Massèra and Vitale: "che."